SCIENCE

DICTIONARY

Compiled by Ralph Hancock

Illustrated by Brian Hoskin, Steven Johnston,
Colin Paine and Peter Rutherford

HENDERSON
PUBLISHING PLC

©1994 HENDERSON PUBLISHING PLC

A

a-, an- in front of a word means 'not'; for example aspheric, not shaped like a sphere

abacus the earliest calculator: frame with beads sliding on wires to represent numbers

abdomen hind section of animal's body; in a vertebrate it contains the guts, in an insect it is the round part at the rear end

aberration distortion of image produced by a lens or mirror, caused by its shape or material

absolute zero lowest possible temperature, -273 °C (see kelvin)

acceleration increase in speed over a given time; measured in metres per second per second (m/s^2)

accelerator particle device for making subatomic particles move at very high speed

accumulator rechargeable electric battery (below)

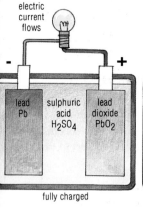

electric current flows

no current

− +

lead
Pb

sulphuric acid
H_2SO_4

lead dioxide
PbO_2

lead sulphate
$PbSO_4$

water
H_2O

lead sulphate
$PbSO_4$

fully charged

completely run down

acetate substance made by treating cellulose; used for plastics and fabrics

acetic acid (CH_3COOH) acid found in vinegar; also used to make acetate

acetylene (C_2H_2) flammable gas used in cutting and welding torches

acid compound containing hydrogen which releases hydrogen ions into water; strong acids taste sour and are corrosive

acoustics science of sound

acrylic resin used in plastics such as Perspex, and fabrics and paints

actinides group of elements similar to actinium (see periodic table)

actinium (Ac, atomic no. 89) element, a radioactive metal

acute of an angle: less than 90°

aerial device which gives out or takes in radio signals

aerobic breathing air; some bacteria are aerobic (see anaerobic)

aerodynamics science of the flow of air or gas

higher speed, lower pressure

air flow

lower speed, higher pressure

aerofoil shape which creates lift when air flows past it, for instance an aircraft wing (see also Bernoulli's law)

aerosol specks of solid or liquid in a gas, for example mist (water in air) or smoke (specks of soot in air)

agar jelly made from seaweed; used by scientists to grow bacteria on

aileron movable panel at rear edge of aircraft wing to tilt the plane

air mixture of 78% nitrogen, 21% oxygen and 1% other gases, mostly carbon dioxide and inert gases

alchemy forerunner of chemistry, mixed with mysticism; alchemists tried to turn metals into gold

alcohol any of a large number of compounds containing one or more hydroxyl (-OH) group; ethanol (or ethyl alcohol, C_2H_5OH) is the kind in alcoholic drinks

aldehyde organic compound related to alcohols and carboxylic acids; the simplest is formaldehyde (HCHO), used to preserve tissue samples and make plastics

alga (plural algae) organism similar to but simpler than plant, including seaweed and pond scum

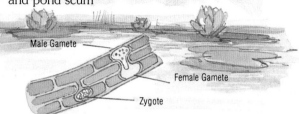

Male Gamete

Female Gamete

Zygote

alkali compound which releases a hydroxyl ion (-OH) when dissolved in water; often corrosive; an example is caustic soda (sodium hydroxide, NaOH); all alkalis are bases (see base)

alkali metals, alkaline earth metals two groups of elements (see periodic table); some of their compounds are alkalis

alkaloid one of many slightly alkaline compounds made by plants; some are poisons (strychnine), others useful (morphine)

allotropy ability of an element to exist in two forms: diamond, graphite and buckminster-fullerene are allotropes of carbon, all quite different but all containing nothing but carbon atoms

alloy mixture of two metals, generally harder or tougher than a pure metal: brass is an alloy of copper and zinc

alpha particle group of two protons and two neutrons, given off by radioactive elements

alternating current (AC) flow of electricity which changes its direction regularly, usually many times a second; mains electricity is AC

alternator electrical generator producing alternating current

altimeter instrument measuring height above sea or ground level

alumina (Al_2O_3) aluminium oxide; many minerals are forms of this, including bauxite (aluminium ore), emery (used as an abrasive) and corundum (sapphire and ruby)

aluminium (Al, atomic no. 13) element, a light silver-white metal; used to build lightweight structures and made into foil ('silver paper')

amalgam alloy with mercury; silver amalgam is used for filling teeth

americium (Am, atomic no. 95) element, a radioactive metal; used in laboratories as a source of neutrons

amine chemical like ammonia but with one of the hydrogen atoms replaced with some group of atoms; the smell of fish is due to amines

amino acid compound of which proteins are made; there are 20 common types

ammeter instrument for measuring electric current

ammonia (NH_3) strong smelling gas which easily dissolves in water; used in commercial refrigerators and to make fertilisers and explosives; household ammonia is a solution in water

amoeba small single celled animal; one kind causes dysentery

amorphous without a crystal structure (see crystal, glass)

ampere (A, amp.) unit of electric current

amphibian type of cold-blooded animal living partly in water: frogs, toads, newts

amplifier device to increase strength of a signal, for instance the electrical signal in a radio set

amplitude height of a wave, including an electromagnetic wave such as a radio wave

amplitude modulation (AM) way of broadcasting a sound radio signal, in which the shape of sound waves is used to change the amplitude of the basic 'carrier' radio waves; in TV broadcasting the picture information is put on to the carrier in the same way (see frequency modulation)

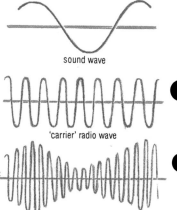

sound wave

'carrier' radio wave

sound wave changes amplitude (height) of carrier wave

anaerobic not breathing air; anaerobic bacteria live in places where there is no air (see aerobic)

anaesthetic causing loss of feeling; or a substance which does this

analgesic relieving pain; or a substance which does this

analogue of a signal: able to have any value between minimum and maximum; opposite of digital

analysis breaking something down into its parts so that they can be identified

anemometer instrument for measuring wind speed, or any air or gas flow

aneroid of a barometer or altimeter: worked by changes in air pressure changing the shape of a sealed metal box with a vacuum inside

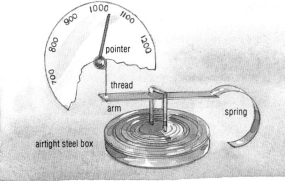

angstrom (Å) ten thousand millionth of a metre (10^{-10} m)

anhydrous containing no water

anneal to slowly cool hot metal or glass to get rid of stresses inside it which might weaken it

annelid animal made up of rings, for instance an earthworm

anode positive electrode, for example in an electric cell

anodizing process of electrolysis used to build up a smooth protective layer of oxide on the surface of aluminium

Antarctic circle circle around Earth 66 degrees 32 minutes south of equator; inside this area the sun never sets at midsummer and never rises at midwinter (see axis)

antenna sense organ of an insect; or another word for aerial, always used in the USA

anthropoids group of animals shaped like people: monkeys, apes and humans

antibiotic killing bacteria; or a drug which does this

antibody substance in the body which recognises a bacterium, virus etc. and starts an attack on it

antigen anything that triggers the action of an antibody

antimatter opposite of real matter; instead of protons, neutrons and electrons it has antiprotons, antineutrons and positrons; when it meets normal matter the two vanish in a burst of energy

antimony (Sb, atomic no. 51) element, a bluish-white metal; used in alloys and electronics; kohl, used as eye make-up, is antimony sulphide

antinode point in a standing wave where there is the most movement

antiseptic preventing growth of bacteria; or a substance which does this

anus end of animal's gut, through which waste products pass out of the body

aperture width of a camera lens; adjusted by sliding metal sheets (iris diaphragm) to vary the amount of light passing through it

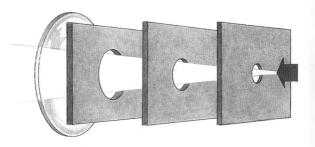

aphelion outermost point of a planet's orbit around the Sun

apogee outermost point of a satellite's orbit around the Earth

aqueous to do with water, for example an aqueous solution, something dissolved in water

arachnids group of animals which includes spiders, scorpions and mites

arc (electric) stream of electric current jumping through the air between two electrodes

Archimedes' principle an object in water is pushed up by a force equal to the weight of water it displaces

Arctic circle circle around Earth 66 degrees 32 minutes north of equator; inside this area the sun never sets at midsummer and never rises at midwinter (see axis)

argon (Ar, atomic no. 18) element, an inert gas found in air; used in light bulbs to stop the filament from burning away

aromatic compound any compound related to benzene; they often have a distinctive smell

arsenic (As, atomic no. 33) element, a metalloid; very poisonous

artery blood vessel carrying blood away from the heart

arthropod type of animal with a hard outside and jointed legs; includes insects, arachnids, crustaceans

asbestos natural mineral, a calcium and magnesium silicate; heat resistant, and so used for fireproofing

asphalt black, sticky solid form of petroleum; used to make roads and to waterproof roofs (see bitumen)

astatine (At, atomic no. 85) element, a radioactive halogen

astronomy science of heavenly bodies; not the same as astrology, which is a kind of fortune telling

atmosphere gases surrounding a planet or other heavenly body

atmospheric pressure pressure caused by the weight of the atmosphere; on average 100 newtons per square metre, varying with the weather

atom smallest unit of an element which is still recognizable as that element; a piece of pure copper is made up of copper atoms

atomic clock very accurate clock using the vibration of atoms as a timer

atomic number number of protons in nucleus of an atom (see periodic table and diagram below)

atomic weight weight of an atom compared to carbon, which is assumed to be 12; this is roughly the average number of protons and neutrons in the nucleus

ATP adenosine triphosphate; the substance in living things which carries energy

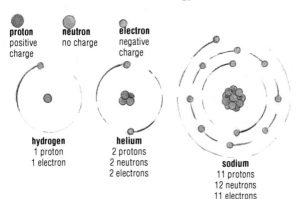

proton
positive charge

neutron
no charge

electron
negative charge

hydrogen
1 proton
1 electron

helium
2 protons
2 neutrons
2 electrons

sodium
11 protons
12 neutrons
11 electrons

audio- in front of a word means 'hearing'

audio frequency frequency of sound which we can hear, between 20 and 20,000 hertz

aurora borealis coloured lights in northern sky caused by streams of charged particles from the Sun

autoclave large pressure cooker for sterilizing food containers, hospital instruments etc.

avionics electronic devices used in or for aircraft

axis pivot (real or imaginary) line around which a revolving object turns; the Earth's axis is tilted at 23 degrees 28 minutes to the plane of its orbit

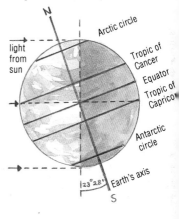

azimuth angle measured around the horizon from the north

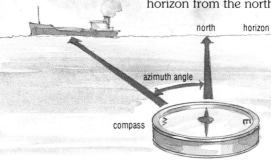

bacillus a stick-shaped bacterium

bacterium (plural bacteria) very small living thing consisting of a single cell; some are useful: bacteria in your guts help digestion, others make cheese and yoghurt but others cause diseases

balance a weighing machine

balance wheel wheel in a mechanical watch or small clock which turns back and forth to keep time

ballistics science of projectiles; things that are thrown, such as bullets and balls

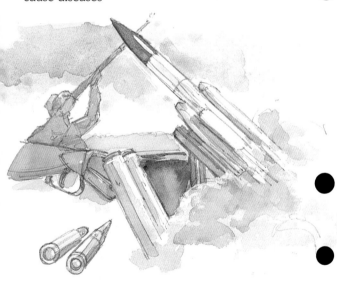

bar (b) unit of pressure; 1 bar is roughly the average pressure of the air; weather forecasts give pressures in millibars (mb)

bar magnet magnet in the shape of a straight bar

barium (Ba, atomic no. 56) element, a heavy metal; it shows up clearly in X-ray pictures, so patients with stomach trouble are given a barium compound to eat before being X-rayed

barometer instrument for measuring air pressure two types: an upright tube full of mercury, and aneroid (see aneroid)

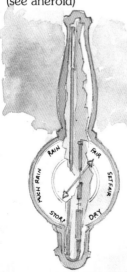

baryon a particle such as a proton or neutron, consisting of three quarks

base (chemistry) compound which reacts with an acid to form a salt and water; all alkalis are bases (see also DNA)

base (mathematics) number used as the basis of counting: ordinary (decimal) numbers use 10 as a base; binary numbers used in computers have a base of 2; they use only two digits, 0 and 1, so you count 0, 1, 10, 11, 100, 101, 110, 111, 1000 …

battery several electrical cells connected together; strictly, a 1.5 volt 'battery' is a cell and a 4.5 volt battery (three 1.5 volt cells) is really a battery

beam radiation of any kind travelling in a particular direction

bearing (engineering) part of a machine which helps it to move smoothly

bearing (mathematics) direction measured as an angle clockwise from north: for example, 270° is due east

becquerel (Bq) unit for measuring radioactivity given off by a material

benzene hydrocarbon (C_6H_6) used as a solvent and in unleaded petrol; causes cancer

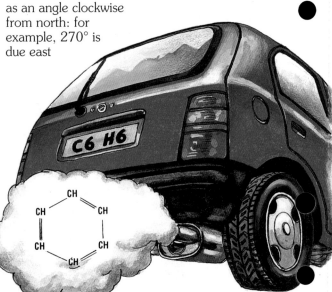

berkelium (Bk, atomic no. 97) element, a radioactive metal; not found in nature, made in a particle accelerator

beryllium (Be, atomic no. 4) element, a light metal; used in alloys

beta radiation electrons given off by radioactive substances

bi- in front of a word means 'two'; for example biconvex, convex on both sides

bicarbonate carbonate including some hydrogen (modern name is hydrogen carbonate), for example sodium bicarbonate ($NaHCO_3$)

'big bang' theory belief that the universe started with a huge explosion and has been spreading out ever since; eventually it may stop spreading and fall back on itself

bilateral symmetry having one half that is a mirror image of the other, as most animals do, but not plants

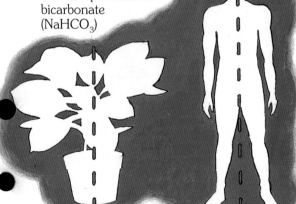

bimetallic strip strip of two layers of different metals that expand different amounts when heated, which makes the strip bend; used in thermostats

billion usually a thousand million; in Britain this used to mean a million million

binary see base (mathematics)

binocular vision seeing with both eyes; a pair of binoculars is two telescopes, one for each eye

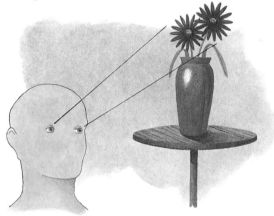

binomial system scientific way of classifying species of living things with two names for genus and species, always written in italics with a capital for the genus only: Quercus robur, an oak tree; Canis lupus, a wolf

bio- at the start of a word means 'life'

biochemistry science of chemical processes in living things

biodegradable able to rot - biodegradable plastics disappear when thrown away, ordinary ones hang around for ever

bioengineering using living things such as bacteria to make useful substances

biogas gas produced by rotting rubbish, which can be used as a fuel

biology science of living things

biomass total weight of animals and/or plants in a certain place

biota all the living things in a place

biped animal with two feet

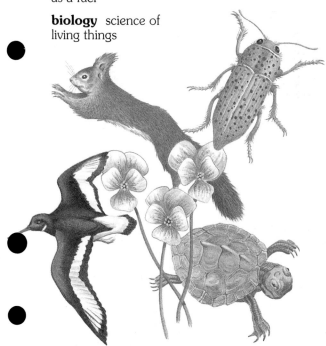

bismuth (Bi, atomic no. 83) element, a light metal; used in alloys with lead which have a very low melting point and are used in fire detectors

bit (computing) single number used in the binary system of counting; it can be 0 or 1 (see base (mathematics))

bitumen black, sticky substance similar to asphalt but usually made from coal

black hole remains of a large star that has collapsed to a small size; it is so dense and heavy that nothing, not even light, can escape from it

blast furnace furnace used to smelt iron ore; it is filled with ore, coke and limestone and air is blasted through; molten iron runs out through a hole at the base

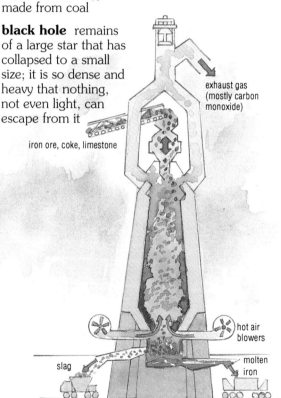

iron ore, coke, limestone

exhaust gas (mostly carbon monoxide)

hot air blowers

slag

molten iron

bleach substance used to whiten cloth, paper etc.; chlorine and calcium oxychloride ($CaOCl_2$) are often used

blind spot part of the retina in the eye where the nerve is attached

blood liquid in animals which carries oxygen, food and waste products around the body

blood group group of people with blood of a particular type; there are four main groups, A, B, AB and O, which must be matched when giving transfusions; but O blood can be given to anyone

boiling point temperature at which a liquid turns to a gas; the boiling point of water, at which it turns to steam, is 100 °C

bond link between two atoms when they form a compound; main kinds are ionic bonds, when one atom 'lends' an electron to another, and covalent bonds, when two atoms share one or more pairs of electrons

sodium (Na)
1 electron in outermost shell

chlorine (Cl)
7 electrons in outermost shell

IONIC BOND

+ **−**

sodium chloride (NaCl)
both outermost shells now have 8 electrons

bone living framework of calcium phosphate ($Ca_3(PO_4)_2$) and collagen; stronger for its weight than steel

boron (B, atomic no. 5) element, a metalloid; used for hardening steel and to shut down atomic reactors by absorbing neutrons

botany science of plants

brake horsepower power of an engine tested with a brake dynamometer

brass alloy of copper and zinc, and sometimes other metals

brazing joining pieces of metal with molten brass

bronze alloy of copper and tin, and sometimes other metals

Brownian movement visible movement of specks of dust in water, caused by water molecules moving

bryophytes group of small plants including mosses

buckminsterfullerene ('buckyballs') form of carbon with atoms arranged to make a hollow ball; commonest kinds have 60 or 70 atoms per ball

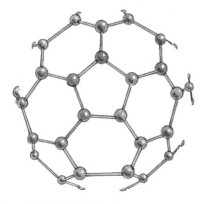

buffer (chemistry) substance that keeps the pH of a mixture constant when acid or alkali is added to it

buffer (computer) temporary store of information which allows, for example, a printer being sent text by a computer to print at its own speed

Bunsen burner gas burner used in laboratories

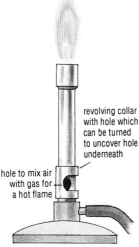

revolving collar with hole which can be turned to uncover hole underneath

hole to mix air with gas for a hot flame

burette glass tube with scale marked on side and tap at bottom, used for pouring measured amounts

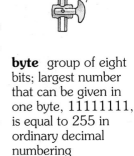

tap

byte group of eight bits; largest number that can be given in one byte, 11111111, is equal to 255 in ordinary decimal numbering

cadmium (Cd, atomic no. 48) element, a bright metal; used to plate steel and to shut down atomic reactors by absorbing neutrons

caesium (Cs, atomic no. 55) element, a soft metal; used in photoelectric cells

calcium (Ca, atomic no. 20) element, a metal; very common in the form of calcium carbonate ($CaCO_3$) as limestone and chalk (see also bone)

calculus branch of mathematics dealing with variables and their rates of change

californium (Cf, atomic no. 98) element, a radioactive metal; not found in nature, made in a particle accelerator

calorie amount of heat needed to raise temperature of 1 g of water by 1 °C; the Calorie used for food is 1000 calories

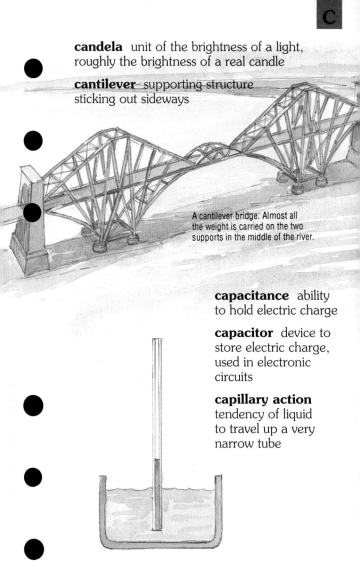

candela unit of the brightness of a light, roughly the brightness of a real candle

cantilever supporting structure sticking out sideways

A cantilever bridge. Almost all the weight is carried on the two supports in the middle of the river.

capacitance ability to hold electric charge

capacitor device to store electric charge, used in electronic circuits

capillary action tendency of liquid to travel up a very narrow tube

C

carat unit of weight for jewels, 200 milligrams; or measure of purity of gold - 24 carat gold is pure

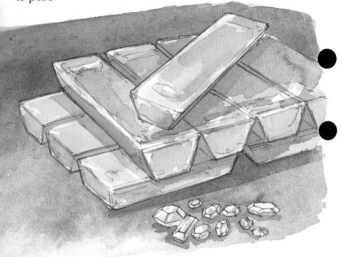

carbide compound of carbon and a metal; for example calcium carbide (CaC_2)

carbohydrate compound consisting mainly of carbon, hydrogen and oxygen; for example sugar or cellulose

carbon (C, atomic no. 6) element, a non-metal; has three allotropes (forms), diamond, graphite and buckminsterfullerene; carbon compounds are the main materials of all living things

carbon cycle natural process in which animals and fires give out carbon while plants take it in (see next entry)

carbon dioxide (CO_2) gas produced by animals breathing and by burning carbon compounds; plants take it in (see photosynthesis)

carbon monoxide (CO) poisonous gas produced by burning carbon compounds with not enough oxygen

carbonate compound of a metal, carbon and oxygen; for example calcium carbonate ($CaCO_3$)

carboxylic acid any organic acid containing a carboxyl group COOH; for example methanoic acid (HCOOH) in nettle stings and ant bites

carcinogen substance that causes cancer

C

carnivore meat-eating animal

carrier wave radio wave with more or less constant frequency to which the signal is added (see amplitude modulation, frequency modulation)

cast iron iron containing 24% carbon; hard and brittle

catalyst a substance which speeds up a chemical reaction but is not used up in the process

cathode negative electrode, for example in an electric cell

cathode ray tube (CRT) glass tube with cathode at the back which gives off a stream of electrons; these travel to the front, hit a layer of fluorescent material and make it glow; a television tube is an example

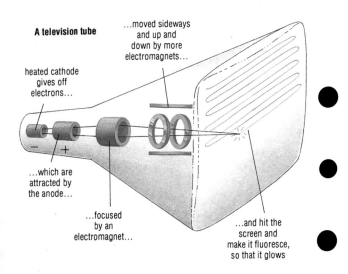

A television tube

...moved sideways and up and down by more electromagnets...

heated cathode gives off electrons...

...which are attracted by the anode...

...focused by an electromagnet...

...and hit the screen and make it fluoresce, so that it glows

caustic corrosive to living things; for example caustic soda (sodium hydroxide, NaOH), an alkali which 'burns' the skin

cell (biology) basic unit of living things; a small, tough 'bag' containing liquid in which the working parts of the cell float; the smallest animals and plants consist of a single cell

cell (electric) a device which creates electric current through a chemical reaction; often wrongly called a battery (see also accumulator)

cellulose carbohydrate which is the main material of plants

Celsius scale of temperature: 0 °C (degrees Celsius) is the freezing point of water, 100 °C is the boiling point of water

centi- (c) in front of a word means 'one hundredth', for example centimetre, one hundredth of a metre

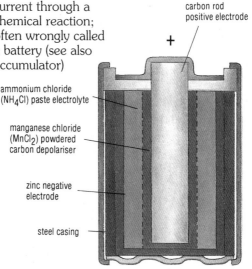

carbon rod positive electrode

+

ammonium chloride (NH$_4$Cl) paste electrolyte

manganese chloride (MnCl$_2$) powdered carbon depolariser

zinc negative electrode

steel casing

centrifugal force
force pulling an object outwards when it is being moved in a circle; caused by inertia, because the object tries to keep going in a straight line - you can feel this when you whirl something around on a string

ceramic material pressed into shape when soft, then baked to harden it

cerium (Ce, atomic no. 58) element, a metal; used in an alloy to make 'flints' for lighters

CFC
(chlorofluorocarbon) type of chemical used in refrigerators, aerosol sprays, as a cleaner and in many other ways; now being phased out, as it destroys ozone in the upper atmosphere

chain reaction
reaction which starts with one event which leads to more events and spreads until all the materials are used up; this can be a chemical reaction or a nuclear one (see fission)

character letter, number or symbol, for example on a computer screen

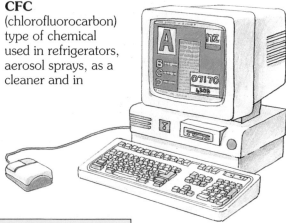

charge quantity of electricity on surface of an object; caused by atoms having more or fewer electrons than normal (more electrons in a negative charge, fewer electrons is a positive charge); opposite charges attract each other, like charges repel

chemistry study of the composition of substances and their effects on one another

chloride compound of a metal with chlorine, for example sodium chloride (common salt, NaCl)

chlorine (Cl, atomic no. 17) element, a greenish poisonous gas; used as a disinfectant and bleach and to make many industrial chemicals

chlorophyll green compound in plants which is the catalyst in photosynthesis

cholesterol fatty substance in blood; necessary, but too much of the wrong kind is harmful

chordate animal with some kind of spinal cord, however simple; includes vertebrates

chromatography method of separating substances in a liquid; one way is to let it soak along a strip of paper

chromium (Cr, atomic no. 24) element, a bright metal; used as a shiny plating for steel (on top of a thicker layer of nickel)

chromosome bundle of DNA in a cell

circuit a circular path; electric current will only flow in a circuit, not to the end of a single wire

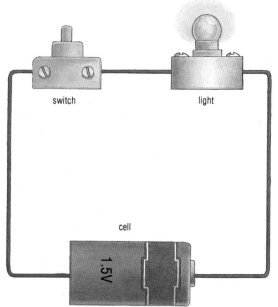

switch

light

cell

1.5V

circumference distance around a circle

clone exact copy of a living thing; for example, a plant grown from a cutting, genetically the same as the original plant

coal gas mixture of gases made by heating coal; mainly hydrogen, methane and carbon monoxide; used as a fuel

cobalt (Co, atomic no. 27) element, a metal similar to iron and which can be magnetized; used in alloys; a radioactive isotope of the element is used as a source of X-rays

coefficient of expansion amount by which a material expands with each 1 °C rise in temperature

coelenterate type of animal including jellyfish and sea anemone

coherent of light or other radiation: having a single wavelength with all the waves in step

collagen tough protein forming much of the structure of the body

colloid mixture of very small particles of one substance in another; many foods are colloids

colour sensation caused by the wavelength of light, or a mixture of different wavelengths; longer waves make us see red, shorter ones blue

compass a magnetic compass is a small needle on a pivot, which always points towards the north pole of the Earth (see also gyrocompass)

complementary colours two colours which, when mixed together, make white; for example red and green

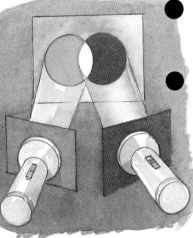

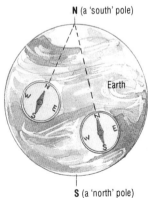

N (a 'south' pole)

Earth

S (a 'north' pole)

compound substance made of two or more elements whose atoms are held together by bonds, so that the numbers of atoms are in a strict ratio; for example in water, H_2O, there are always two hydrogen atoms to each oxygen atom (see also mixture)

concave having a surface with a hollow shape; a magnifying mirror is concave

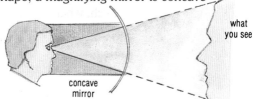

what you see

concave mirror

condensation turning from a gas to a liquid

conduction allowing electricity or heat to pass through; a substance that does this is a conductor

conservation of energy a basic law of science: energy cannot be created or destroyed; it just changes from one form to another (but in nuclear reactions, energy can turn into matter and back)

conservation of matter a basic law of science: matter cannot be created or destroyed; it just changes from one form to another (but see just above)

constant quantity that does not change in a mathematical calculation

contact piece of metal touching another piece to carry electric current across

continuum something that goes on without a break; for example space and time

convection carrying heat in a flow of a liquid or gas

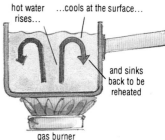

hot water rises... ...cools at the surface...

and sinks back to be reheated

gas burner

convex with a bulging surface; a magnifying glass has a convex lens

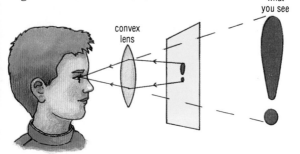

copper (Cu, atomic no. 29) element, a brownish metal; conducts electricity well, used in wiring; also made into alloys brass and bronze

core of the Earth: the central part, mostly made of iron and nickel

corrosion of metals: combining with oxygen or other substances so that the surface becomes covered with a compound; oxygen corrodes iron to form iron oxide (Fe_2O_3), which is rust

cosine see trigonometry

cosmic rays radiation hitting the Earth from outer space (not from the Sun)

cosmology theories about the nature of the Universe

coulomb (C) amount of electricity when 1 ampere flows for 1 second

cracking breaking up a compound by heating it; method used in oil refining

critical angle shallowest angle at which a ray of light hitting the surface of a transparent object will go through it; beyond this angle all the light reflects off the surface

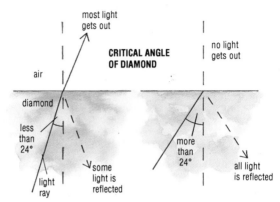

CRITICAL ANGLE OF DIAMOND

most light gets out

no light gets out

air

diamond

less than 24°

some light is reflected

light ray

more than 24°

all light is reflected

critical mass minimum amount of nuclear fuel needed before reaction can begin

crucible heatproof container for high-temperature chemical processes

crust rocks which form the outer layer of the Earth

crustacean type of arthropod including crabs, lobsters and shrimps

crystal solid substance in which atoms are arranged in neat rows

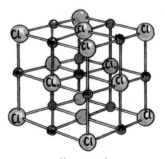

crystallography science of crystal structure

cube (mathematics) number multiplied by itself twice

curing hardening of an adhesive or other material

curium (Cm, atomic no. 96) element, a radioactive metal; not found in nature, made in a particle accelerator

current flow of electricity, caused by electrons moving through a material

cybernetics science of control and communication

cycle in any repeated action, one complete repetition; for example, the frequency of a wave is the number of cycles per second

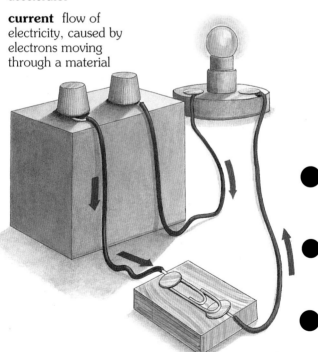

damping slowing down movement, for example reducing vibration

data (plural) information

dead reckoning estimating your position only from the time and direction of your journey

decay (radioactive) breaking up of radioactive atoms; they turn to atoms of other elements, at the same time emitting radiation

deci- (d) in front of a word means 'one tenth'

decibel (dB) unit used to compare loudness of sounds; a sound 10 dB louder than another is twice as loud

decimal see base (mathematics)

declination angle of a star, etc. above the equator

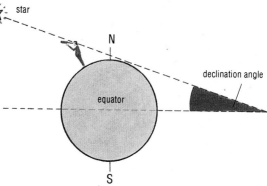

decomposition of a compound: breaking up permanently into simpler parts

degree (°) unit of temperature and of angle

dehydration removal of water

denominator number below the line in a fraction, for example in $\frac{1}{2}$ the denominator is 2

density mass of a substance compared with that of water:

1 cm³ of water weighs 1 g, 1 cm³ of gold weighs 19.3 g, so the density of gold is 19.3

detonator device for setting off an explosion

deuterium isotope of hydrogen with a neutron in the nucleus as well as a proton

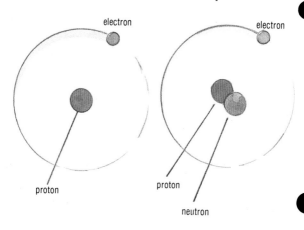

electron

proton

hydrogen

electron

proton

neutron

deuterium

dew point temperature at which moisture in the air begins to condense; the moister the air, the higher the dew point

di- in front of a word means 'two'; for example dioxide, with two oxygen atoms

dia- in front of a word means 'through'

dialysis filtering a liquid with a semi-permeable membrane; used to purify blood of people with damaged kidneys

diameter line across circle, cutting it in half

diaphragm thin sheet of material; for example, in a microphone, where sound makes the diaphragm vibrate

(see also iris diaphragm)

die shaping device; for example, hole through which metal is pulled to make wire, or block for stamping design on a coin

diesel engine without spark plugs; it works by compressing the fuel mixture until this explodes by itself

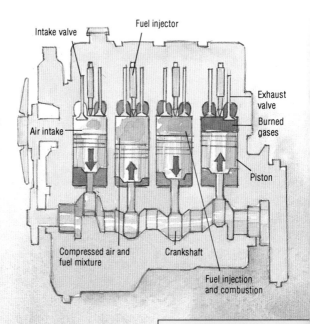

Intake valve

Fuel injector

Exhaust valve

Burned gases

Air intake

Piston

Compressed air and fuel mixture

Crankshaft

Fuel injection and combustion

diffraction spreading out of waves as they pass by an object

diffusion mixing or spreading out; smoke diffuses through the air

digestion breaking down food in the body to get useful substances

digit single number symbol: 91 is a number of two digits

digital of a signal: able to have only certain values, such as on and off; opposite of analogue

dimension a mathematical power connected with measurement: a solid object has three dimensions, height, width and length; speed has two dimensions, length and time (for example miles per hour)

diode electronic device which will only let current through in one direction

dioptre measurement of strength of a lens; reciprocal of the focal length in metres: a lens with a focal length of 0.25 m, that is $1/4$ m, is 4 dioptres

dip angle between Earth's magnetic field and horizontal; a compass needle hung on a thread will tilt to this angle

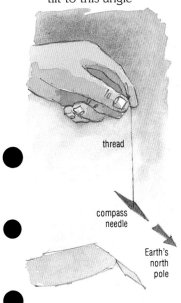

thread

compass needle

Earth's north pole

direct current (DC) steady flow of electricity in one direction, as from a battery

disc (or disk) used for recording a signal: on an audio disc the signal is recorded as a zigzag groove in the shape of the sound wave; on a compact disc the signal is recorded in digital form as a row of tiny pits which are read with a laser; on a computer disc the signal is also digital, but is recorded as magnetic areas on a plastic disc coated with magnetic material

discharge tube tube containing gas which glows when electric current passes through it; for example a fluorescent lamp

discrete separate; the dots in this line .... are discrete

disinfectant able to kill bacteria; a substance which does this

disperse phase the small specks of matter in a colloid

dispersion medium; the part of a colloid in which the disperse phase is scattered

displacement weight of water pushed aside by an object in the water

dissociation of a compound: breaking up into simpler parts which can be rejoined

distillation separating a mixture of liquids by heating, so that one liquid boils off and can be condensed in a separate container

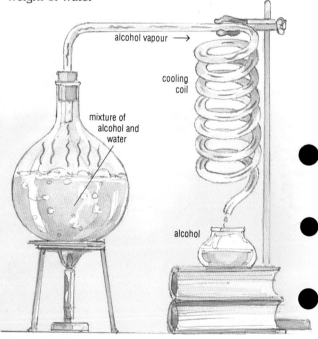

alcohol vapour ⟶

cooling coil

mixture of alcohol and water

alcohol

distortion (electronics) change in the wave shape of a signal; usually unwanted

DNA (deoxyribose nucleic acid) substance in a living cell or virus which carries the information for making new cells or viruses; a molecule shaped like a twisted rope ladder, with 'rungs' which are pairs of bases; the information is stored in the order of the bases (see also RNA)

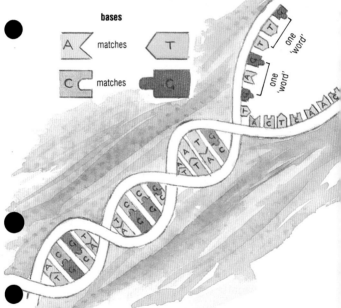

bases

A matches T

C matches G

one 'word'

one 'word'

dominant of a gene: causing an effect when it is inherited from only one parent

doping adding very small amounts of extra substances to semiconductors to change their behaviour

Doppler effect difference in pitch of sound made by an object when it is approaching or going away; the pitch of a police car siren falls as the car goes past; also happens with light (see red shift)

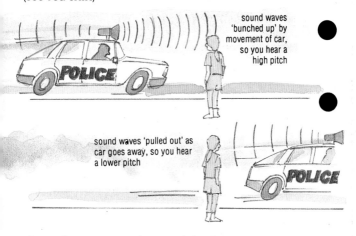

sound waves 'bunched up' by movement of car, so you hear a high pitch

sound waves 'pulled out' as car goes away, so you hear a lower pitch

drag friction caused by an aircraft moving through the air

dry ice frozen carbon dioxide; used to keep things very cold

ductile able to be pulled out into a long shape; a ductile metal can be made into a wire

dynamics science of moving objects

and the forces acting on them

dynamometer device for measuring forces; for example, a brake dynamometer which measures the power of an engine by making it turn against a brake and measuring the force on the brake

dysprosium (Dy, atomic no. 66) element, a metal

earthing making an electrical contact with the ground; electrical devices are earthed to stop current going through your body to the ground, which would give you a shock

echinoderm type of animal including starfish and sea urchin; all have radial symmetry

echo sounding finding how far away an object is by bouncing a sound off it and timing how long the sound takes to come back

eclipse darkness when the Moon is passing in front of the Sun; or when the Earth's shadow falls on the Moon

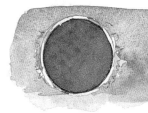

ecology science of plants and animals in the environment

ecosystem set of living things in a particular place

E

efficiency of a machine: ratio of the amount of energy got out of a machine (as work) to the amount put in (as fuel); written as a percentage

egg sex cell of a female animal (including animals that give birth to live young)

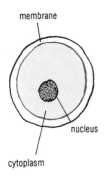

membrane

nucleus

cytoplasm

einsteinium (Es, atomic no. 99) element, a radioactive metal; not found in nature, made in a particle accelerator

elasticity ability of something to return to its original shape

after being squeezed or pulled

electricity general word for events caused by electrons when they are not attached to atoms

electrode piece of metal or carbon through which an electric current enters or leaves a liquid or a gas

electrolysis causing a chemical reaction by passing an electric current through a liquid

electrolyte liquid through which electric current passes; this includes the liquid in the cells of a living creature

electromagnet temporary magnet whose magnetic attraction is caused by an electric current flowing in a coil of wire; unlike a permanent magnet it can be switched off

electromagnetic radiation wide range of radiation, from gamma rays through light to radio waves; it is carried by particles called photons, which can travel through space, but mysteriously at the same time it consists of waves whose wavelength determines what kind of radiation it is

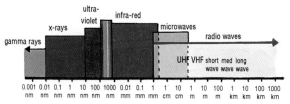

electron tiny negatively charged particle which orbits the nucleus (centre) of an atom but can be removed from it; atoms lose and gain electrons in chemical reactions; a flow of electrons is an electric current

electron microscope microscope using a beam of electrons instead of light, which allows much smaller objects to be seen

electron shell a layer of electrons in orbit around the nucleus of an atom; each shell can only hold a certain number of electrons and the shells fill up from the bottom; the first three shells can hold 2, 8 and 8 electrons; an atom whose outermost shell is full is stable and unlikely to take part in a chemical reaction, but one with a partly filled shell is unstable and likely to react (see the first 18 elements in the periodic table, where the atomic number is also the number of electrons)

electronic using electric current in a precise, controlled way, especially to carry information

electroplating using an electric current to cover one metal with a layer of another

electroscope simple device for detecting an electric charge, in which a piece of gold leaf stands up when there is a charge

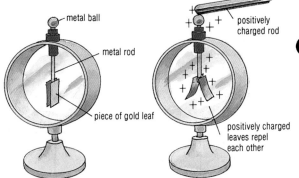

metal ball

metal rod

piece of gold leaf

positively charged rod

positively charged leaves repel each other

electrostatics science of static electricity

element substance consisting of only one kind of atom

elevator of aircraft: hinged surface on horizontal part of tail, which is moved up or down to make the plane climb or dive

embryo young unborn animal at a very early stage of growth; also the part inside a seed which turns into a plant

emulsion tiny drops of one liquid suspended in another; milk is an emulsion of oil in water; the 'emulsion' on photographic film has been allowed to dry

energy ability to do work; this can be in many forms: heat, electrical energy, mechanical energy (in a moving object), chemical energy (in a fuel that can be burnt) etc. (see also kinetic, potential energy)

energy state one of the orbits in which electrons around an atom can be; if energy is put into an atom this can bump up an electron to a higher state; when the electron drops back to a lower state, the atom gives out energy - this is what happens in fluorescence

entropy an increase in randomness; for example when a cup of tea cools the heat energy spreads out into the room, and you cannot get it back into the tea

enzyme a natural catalyst in a living thing; all enzymes are proteins

equation mathematical statement that two things are equal

equator line running around the Earth halfway between the north and south poles

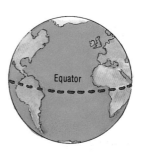

Equator

equinox time in spring and autumn when day and night are the same length

erbium (Er, atomic no. 68) element, a metal; used in lasers

ergonomics science of making things easier and more comfortable to use

ester type of substance formed by reaction between an acid and an organic compound; many esters have a fruity smell; for example ethyl ethanoate ($CH_3COOC_2H_5$), used as nail polish remover

ether type of substance formed by linking two alcohol molecules; diethyl ether ($C_2H_5OC_2H_5$) is used as an anaesthetic

etching applying acid to a surface to eat it away; parts that are not to be etched are given an acid-proof coating called a resist; used in the making of microchips

europium (Eu, atomic no. 63) element, a metal

evolution change of form in a species of living thing, caused by natural selection - creatures most suited to their environment have more descendants

excitation adding energy to an atom (see energy state)

experimenter effect accidental change in the result of an experiment caused by observing it: taking a sample from an object makes it smaller; watching animals makes them behave differently, etc.

exponent (mathematics) small raised number used to show the power to which a number is raised; 10^2 is 10 to the power of 2, or 10 x 10

extrusion forcing a material through a small hole to shape it; used to make rods and tubes

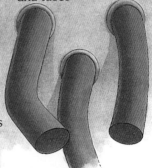

f number
measurement of how much light gets through a camera lens; the focal length divided by the aperture

factor number which divides exactly into another number; the factors of 6 are 1, 2, 3 and 6

faeces solid waste products of an animal

Fahrenheit obsolete scale of temperature: water freezes at 32 degrees Fahrenheit (32 °F) and boils at 212 °F

farad unit of electrical capacitance

fatigue brittle state of metal caused by repeated bending; if the metal is bent again it will snap

fat solid greasy substance in animals and plants; animals use fat as a food store and a heat insulator; oil is a similar substance but liquid

fatty acid type of organic acid; fats and oils are made of three molecules of various fatty acids joined to a molecule of glycerol

fauna all the animals in a certain place

feedback returning some of the output of a device to its input; this can happen by accident in a PA system when sound from the speakers gets into the microphone, causing a loud howling noise (for another example, see governor)

fermentation chemical change in an organic substance caused by bacteria or yeasts; in winemaking, yeasts ferment sugar in grape juice to make alcohol

fermium (Fm, atomic no. 100) element, a radioactive metal; not found in nature, made in a particle accelerator

fibre optic thin strand of glass used to carry light; telephone signals are often turned into light signals and sent in this way

Light bounces off the inside of the fibre at such a shallow angle that it cannot get out.

field area in which a force is exerted: a magnet has a magnetic field around it, a wire carrying a current has an electric field and a magnetic one

filament a thin strand, such as the wire in a lightbulb

filter anything that will let through some things but not others; for example a sheet of filter paper, or the treble and bass controls on a hi-fi

fission splitting apart; bacteria reproduce by fission

fission (nuclear) process in a nuclear reactor or atom bomb: an atom breaks up, throwing off neutrons which hit more atoms and break them up, producing more neutrons, and so on in a chain reaction; fission of heavy elements such as uranium releases a lot of energy

Neutron enters uranium nucleus...   ...which becomes unstable...   ...and splits, releasing neutrons...   ...which may hit other nuclei.

neutron   nucleus   barium nucleus   krypton nucleus

fix (in plants) some plants have bacteria on their roots which 'fix' (take in) nitrogen from the atmosphere, making nitrogen compounds which the plant feeds on

flora all the plants in a certain place; intestinal flora are the bacteria in the gut, which help to digest food

fluid liquid or gas

fluorescence effect in which a substance takes in energy and sends it out again in the form of light; in a fluorescent lamp, electricity makes gases and other chemicals inside the tube glow (see energy state)

fluoride a compound of fluorine, usually with a metal; sodium fluoride is in drinking water (natural or added) and protects against tooth decay

fluorine (F, atomic no. 9) element, a yellow gas; reacts violently with other elements

F

flux (chemical) substance added to another to make it easier to melt

flux (physics) rate of flow in a particular direction; often used to measure the energy flowing in a magnetic field

focal length distance from convex lens at which the lens will focus parallel rays of light to a point; for a concave lens, which spreads out rays instead of focusing them, this is worked out by drawing the line of the rays back the way they have come until the lines cross

foetus young animal older than an embryo but not yet born

food web (or food chain) in an ecosystem, the pattern of what feeds on what

force something that can change the speed or direction of an object (which includes starting it moving or stopping it)

formula way of writing a mathematical statement or the make-up of a chemical by using symbols: $x^2 + y^2$, H_2SO_4

fossil remains of living thing preserved in rock

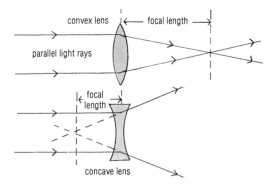

convex lens — focal length →

parallel light rays

focal length

concave lens

fossil fuel coal, oil or natural gas, all of which formed over millions of years from the remains of living things

four-stroke engine engine in which the piston goes up and down twice for every time the mixture explodes

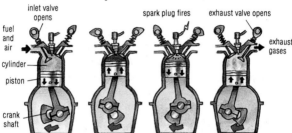

inlet valve opens   spark plug fires   exhaust valve opens

fuel and air

exhaust gases

cylinder

piston

crank shaft

francium (Fr, atomic no. 87) element, a radioactive metal

free of an element: by itself, not part of a compound; there is free oxygen in the atmosphere

freezing point temperature at which a liquid turns to a solid; the freezing point of water, at which it turns to ice, is 0 °C

frequency rate at which something repeats, such as a wave changing direction

frequency modulation (FM) way of broadcasting a sound radio signal, in which the shape of sound waves is used to change the frequency of the basic 'carrier' radio waves; used for high-quality sound broadcasting and for the sound part of a television signal (see amplitude modulation)

friction force that resists movement between two objects touching each other

fructose ($C_6H_{12}O_6$) type of sugar found in flowers, fruit and honey (see glucose)

fuel a substance used to produce energy in the form of heat

fuel cell type of electrical cell which is fed with fuel (usually hydrogen and oxygen) so that it produces electricity for ever; used in spacecraft

fulcrum pivot point of a lever

fungus (plural fungi) plant-like organism which, unlike a true plant or an alga, cannot make its own food by photosynthesis; for example mushrooms, moulds, yeasts

fuse thin wire in an electric circuit; if the current gets dangerously high it heats and melts the fuse, which breaks and shuts the current off

fusion joining together: a sperm fuses with an egg to fertilize it

fusion (nuclear) process in which two atoms join together; fusion of light elements releases a lot of energy, for example when hydrogen atoms fuse to make helium atoms in a star or a hydrogen bomb

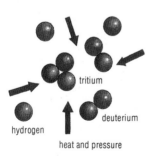

tritium
deuterium
hydrogen
heat and pressure

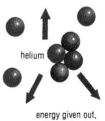

helium
energy given out, adding to heat

g acceleration of a falling object caused by gravity; 9.81 m/s^2

gadolinium (Gd, atomic no. 64) element, a metal

galaxy huge cluster of stars

gallium (Ga, atomic no. 31) element, a metal; the compound gallium arsenide (GaAs) is used to make microchips

galvanizing coating steel with zinc to protect it from rust

galvanometer device for measuring very small electric currents using a magnetic field

gamete a plant or animal cell which takes part in sexual reproduction, for example a sperm or egg cell; it has only half the DNA of a normal cell, so when male and female gametes join there is a complete set

gamma ray electromagnetic radiation with very short wavelength, below 0.01 nm (nanometres); given off by radioactive elements; harmful to living things

gas a substance in which the molecules move about freely and spread out to fill a container

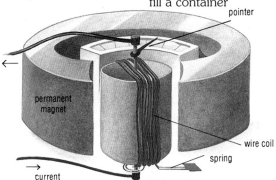

pointer

permanent magnet

wire coil

spring

current

G

gate device in logic circuit: a NOT gate has one input and produces an output only when the input is off; an AND gate has two inputs and produces an output only when both are on; an OR gate produces an output when one or both inputs are on; an XOR gate produces an output only when one input is on and the other off

Geiger-Müller counter device for detecting particles given off by radioactive substances

gel jelly; a colloid in which the solid part has formed a network holding in the liquid

gene section of DNA which carries the information to produce an effect; for example, there is a gene for having brown eyes, and if you do not inherit it you have blue eyes

generator machine which produces electric current when it is turned

genetics science which describes how living things inherit features from their parents, and how they vary

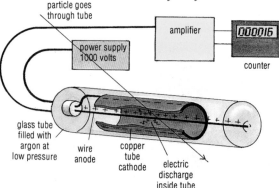

particle goes through tube

amplifier

000016

power supply 1000 volts

counter

glass tube filled with argon at low pressure

wire anode

copper tube cathode

electric discharge inside tube

genome all the DNA in one cell of a living thing

genus group of related species of living thing; the lion (Panthera leo) and tiger (Panthera tigris) belong to the big cat genus Panthera

geodesic line which is the shortest distance between two points on the surface of a sphere; a geodesic dome is made of struts which follow this line

geology science of the Earth's crust

germ vague word for something which causes a disease; might be a bacterium or other small creature, or a virus

germanium (Ge, atomic no. 32) element, a metalloid; used as a semiconductor in many electronic devices

giga- (G) in front of a word means 'a hundred million'; for example gigabyte, 100 million bytes

gland organ which produces a substance that the body needs

glass solid substance in which atoms are not arranged neatly but jumbled up; there are many kinds apart from ordinary window glass, for example asphalt and the hard sugar in boiled sweets (see supercooling)

glass fibre a thin strand of glass; fibres are mixed with plastic to make a light, strong material, glass-reinforced plastic (GRP)

glucose ($C_6H_{12}O_6$) type of sugar found in flowers, fruit and honey, and used as a store of energy in the blood of animals; glucose and fructose have the same formula but the molecule is a different shape

gold (Au, atomic no. 79) element, a heavy metal which does not corrode; used for jewellery and corrosion-proof contacts in electronic circuits

gonad organ that produces gametes in a male or female animal

governor device used to keep an engine from going too fast

graft to join two parts of a living thing; they must be reasonably alike for the graft to succeed

gram (g) unit of weight; kilograms (kg, 1000 g) are used instead in the MKS system of scientific measurement

gravitation force which attracts any two objects together; strength depends on the mass of the objects and their distance apart

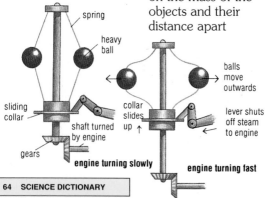

spring

heavy ball

sliding collar

shaft turned by engine

gears

engine turning slowly

balls move outwards

collar slides up ↑

lever shuts off steam to engine

engine turning fast

gravity force due to the Earth's gravitation

gray unit of the amount of radiation someone receives

gypsum calcium sulphate ($CaSO_4.2H_2O$), used for plaster

gyrocompass compass which uses gyroscopes rather than a magnetic needle to keep it pointing in the same direction

gyroscope heavy spinning wheel, which resists if you try to tilt it

habitat place where an animal or plant lives

hadron a particle formed of quarks

haematite natural iron oxide (Fe_2O_3); a common iron ore

haemoglobin red substance in blood which carries oxygen around the body

hafnium (Hf, atomic no. 72) element, a metal; used in an alloy with tungsten to make light bulb filaments

hahnium (Ha, atomic no. 105) element, a radioactive metal; not found in nature, made in a particle accelerator

half life average time taken for half the atoms of a radioactive element to decay into atoms of another element

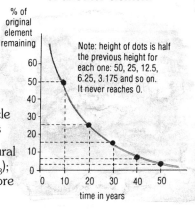

% of original element remaining

Note: height of dots is half the previous height for each one: 50, 25, 12.5, 6.25, 3.175 and so on. It never reaches 0.

time in years

H

halogens group of gases (see periodic table) which react violently with other elements because they have one free space in their outer electron shell

hard water water with calcium and magnesium compounds dissolved in it; this makes soap difficult to lather, and the compounds come out of solution and form 'scale' inside pipes and 'fur' in kettles

harmonic wave added to another wave; the wavelength of the harmonic is an exact fraction ($\frac{1}{2}$, $\frac{1}{3}$ etc.) of that of the first wave; the tone of musical sounds is caused by harmonics (see also octave)

heat a form of energy due to the movement of the atoms in a substance; at any temperature above absolute zero atoms jump about constantly, and the higher the temperature the faster they move

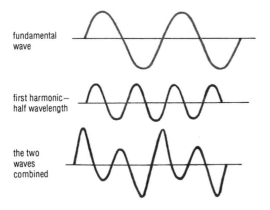

fundamental wave

first harmonic— half wavelength

the two waves combined

heavy water water in which all the hydrogen is in the form of the isotope deuterium; there is very little of this in normal water, and it is extracted for use as a moderator in some nuclear reactors

hect(o)- (H) in front of a word means 'a hundred'; for example hectare, a hundred ares

helium (He, atomic no. 2) element, a light inert gas; used in balloons

helix spiral with a corkscrew shape

herbicide chemical for killing plants

herbivore plant-eating animal

hertz (Hz) unit of frequency: 1 hertz is 1 cycle per second

high tension high voltage

histology study of the tissue of living things

screw

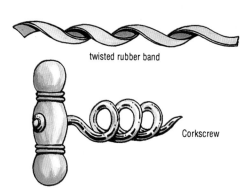
twisted rubber band

Corkscrew

holmium (Ho, atomic no. 67) element, a metal

holograph three-dimensional image made with laser light

hominid like a human: includes humans and their near ancestors from the past few million years

hormone chemical produced by the body in very small amounts to send a message to an organ to make it do something

horsepower (hp) old unit of power still used for cars; 1 hp = 0.75 kilowatts

host creature infested with a parasite

humidity amount of water vapour in the air

hybrid plant or animal with two parents of different species

hydrated containing water (see water of crystallization)

hydraulics use of liquid under pressure to work machines

hydro- in front of a word means 'water' or 'hydrogen'

hydrocarbon compound consisting of hydrogen and carbon only; petroleum and natural gas are mixtures of hydrocarbons

hydrochloric acid (HCl) strong acid; it exists in your stomach, and is used in industry and for etching

hydroelectric power electricity produced by water in rivers etc., used to turn turbines

hydrofoil device which works like a wing underwater to lift a boat out of the water

hydrogen (H, atomic no. 1) the lightest element, a gas, though at very low temperatures it becomes a metal; it is the nuclear fuel of the sun and other stars (see fusion), has many compounds (see carbohydrate, hydrocarbon), and can be burnt as a pollution-free fuel

H

hydrogen peroxide
(H_2O_2) liquid used
as a bleach and
disinfectant, and to
provide oxygen for
rockets

hydrometer
device for measuring
density of a liquid;
used to measure
strength of alcoholic
drinks - alcohol is less
dense than water

hydrophilic
absorbing water

hydrophone
underwater
microphone, as used
by echo sounder

hydroponics
growing plants in
water with fertilizer,
without soil

hypersonic travelling
over five times faster
than sound

hypotenuse longest
side of a right-angled
triangle

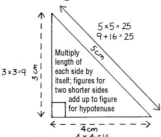

$5 \times 5 = 25$
$9 + 16 = 25$

5 cm

3 cm

$3 \times 3 = 9$

Multiply
length of
each side by
itself; figures for
two shorter sides
add up to figure
for hypotenuse

4 cm
$4 \times 4 = 16$

hypothesis
unproved theory

hygrometer device
for measuring
humidity

igneous of rock: formed from cooled lava or magma; for example granite

image picture of object formed by lens or mirror; a 'real' image can be projected on to a screen, a 'virtual' image can only be seen by looking into the lens or mirror

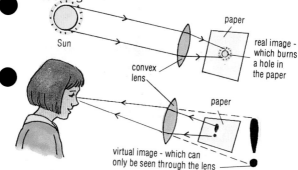

Sun

paper

real image - which burns a hole in the paper

convex lens

paper

virtual image - which can only be seen through the lens

implant to put something in the body of an animal or person; or something put in, for example an artificial hip joint

incident ray ray of light falling on a lens or mirror

indicator chemical which changes colour to show whether a substance is acidic or basic

indium (In, atomic no. 49) element, a soft metal; used for 'doping' microchips

induction creation of an electric current in a wire by changing the magnetic field around it (which can be done by moving a magnet, or by switching a current on or off in a nearby wire); or making an object magnetic by using another magnet

inert gases group of elements (see periodic table) which very seldom react with other elements because they have completely filled outer electron shells

inertia tendency of an object to keep moving at the same speed in the same direction (or, if it is not moving, to stay still)

infra-red radiation electromagnetic radiation with a wavelength slightly longer than that of visible light (700 nm (nanometres) to 1 mm); can be felt as heat

infrasonic of a sound: too low-pitched to hear (less than 20 Hz)

ingot cast metal block which will later be shaped into something

inorganic chemistry science of inorganic compounds

inorganic compounds compounds not containing carbon, plus a few very simple carbon compounds (see organic compounds)

insect type of animal: arthropod with body in three sections, and six legs

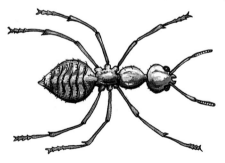

insoluble not able to dissolve in a liquid

insulation stopping heat or electricity from getting through; a material that does this is an insulator

insulin hormone which controls the amount of sugar in the blood

integer whole number: 1, 2, 3 etc.

integrated circuit electric circuit in one piece; for example a microchip

interference effects caused when two sets of waves or patterns overlap; with light waves this creates a stripy pattern

inverse ratio (mathematics) relationship in which an increase in one thing causes a decrease in the other

invertebrate animal with no backbone

iodine (I, atomic no. 53) element, a deep purple solid; used in medicine, chemical analysis and photography

ion atom which has more or fewer electrons than its normal number, so that it has an electric charge; a positive ion has fewer electrons, a negative ion more

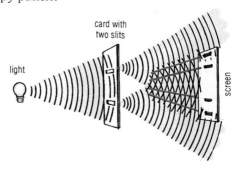

light · card with two slits · screen

I

ionize to add or remove electrons from the atoms of a substance

ionosphere ionized layer in the atmosphere between about 90 and 650 km above the Earth; it reflects radio waves, so that a radio signal can travel around the Earth

VHF and UHF

short wave

200km

medium wave

100km

long wave

radio transmitter

iridium (Ir, atomic no. 77) element, a metal similar to platinum; used with platinum to make hard, wear-resistant alloys

iris diaphragm ring of sliding metal sheets around camera lens, used to control its aperture (width)

iron (Fe, atomic no. 26) element, a strong metal which can be magnetized; used mostly in the form of steel to make all kinds of machines and structures; the red colour of blood is due to an iron compound

iso- in front of a word means 'equal'

isobar line on weather map connecting points of equal pressure

isomer compound with same formula but atoms differently arranged (see glucose for an example)

isotonic of a liquid: having the same concentration as another; an isotonic drink has the same amount of dissolved minerals as your body

isotope a form of an element with the same number of protons but a different number of neutrons from another form; many elements have one common stable isotope and one or more rare unstable, radioactive 'radioisotopes', or all the isotopes may be of this kind; different isotopes are numbered with their atomic weight (uranium-238, uranium-235)

jamming blocking a radio broadcast by transmitting a stronger signal at the same frequency

jet engine engine which takes in air, compresses it, mixes it with fuel and burns the mixture to produce a blast of hot gas

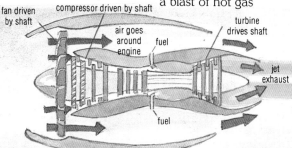

fan driven by shaft

compressor driven by shaft

air goes around engine

fuel

turbine drives shaft

jet exhaust

fuel

jetstream strong wind in upper atmosphere

joule (J) unit of energy and work; the energy in food is measured in kilojoules (1000 J) (see also work)

kaolin china clay; also used to ease stomach upsets by buffering acid

kelvin (K) a unit for measuring temperature: it is the same size as a degree Celsius (°C) but starts at absolute zero (-273 °C); this means that when the temperature of an object rises from 100 K to 200 K there is twice as much heat in it

keratin tough protein found in skin, hair, feathers, nails, claws, hooves etc.

ketone organic compound containing a CO group; for example acetone (propanone, CH_3COCH_3)

kiln industrial furnace

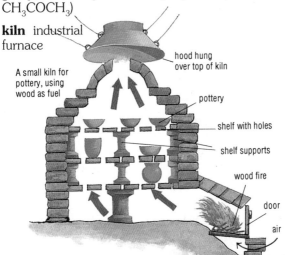

hood hung over top of kiln

A small kiln for pottery, using wood as fuel

pottery

shelf with holes

shelf supports

wood fire

door

air

kilo- (k) in front of a word means 'a thousand'; for example kilometre, a thousand metres

kinetic energy energy that exists in the movement of a moving object (see potential energy)

klystron electronic device for producing microwaves; used in radar

krypton (Kr, atomic no. 36) element, an inert gas; used in fluorescent lamps

kurchatovium see rutherfordium

lactation production of milk by a female mammal

lactose type of sugar found in milk

laminar flow smooth flow of a fluid; opposite of turbulence

lanthanides another name for the rare earth elements, because the series begins with lanthanum (see periodic table)

lanthanum (La, atomic no. 57) element, a metal

larva form in which some animals, such as insects, hatch from an egg; different in shape from the adult; for example a caterpillar

larynx 'voicebox' of an animal, used to make sounds

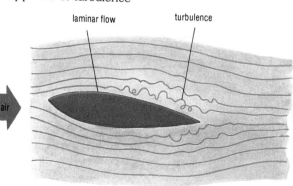

laminar flow   turbulence

air

laser device for producing a narrow, intense beam of coherent light

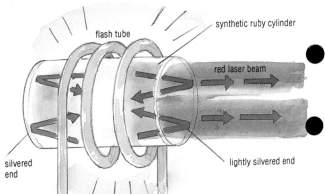

latent hidden but available

latent heat amount of heat needed to melt 1 g of a solid at its melting point, or boil 1 g of a liquid at its boiling point

lathe machine which turns a piece of metal or wood against a cutting blade to cut around shape

latitude position on the Earth's surface measured as an angle north or south of the equator

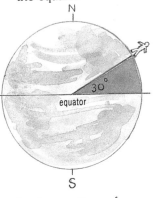

lattice pattern of atoms in a crystal

laughing gas nitrous oxide (N_2O), used as an anaesthetic

lava rock which, in a molten state, has flowed out of a volcano

lawrencium (Lr, atomic no. 103) element, a radioactive metal; not found in nature, made in a particle accelerator

leach to wash out with water; rain leaches fertilizer out of the soil

lead (Pb, atomic no. 82) element, a heavy, soft metal; used in accumulators, as a shield against radiation, for roofing, and alloyed with tin to make solder

lens curved piece of transparent material for bringing rays of light together (convex lens) or spreading them apart (concave lens)

lepton smallest type of particle; for example an electron or a photon; leptons are not made of smaller pieces, as far as we know

leucocyte white blood cell

lever bar with a pivot (called the fulcrum), used to increase the force applied to an object, or to increase the distance it travels

fulcrum (pivot point)

lichen not a plant, but a fungus and an alga working together

light electromagnetic radiation with wavelength between 400 nm (nanometres) and 700 nm; at the shortest wavelength we see violet, at the longest we see red

light-emitting diode (LED) semiconductor device which glows when an electric current goes through it; used for small indicator lights and displays

light meter device for measuring amount of light, using a photoelectric cell; used in cameras

light, speed of (and of all electromagnetic radiation in a vacuum) is 299,792,458 metres per second; nothing can move faster than this

lignite early stage of coal when it is only a few million years old; it is brown and burns with a lot of smoke

lime quicklime is calcium oxide (CaO), a caustic substance made by heating limestone; when water is added it becomes slaked lime, calcium hydroxide ($Ca(OH)_2$), an alkali used to improve acid soil

linear motor electric motor which moves in a straight line rather than turning; used for maglev trains

lipid a fatty or oily substance

liquefaction turning a gas to a liquid by cooling it or compressing it, or both

liquid substance which flows to take on the shape of its container, but does not spread out to fill it entirely

liquid crystal liquid with long molecules which can be lined up with a magnetic field; this can be used to change its appearance, as in liquid crystal displays used in watches and laptop computers

lithium (Li, atomic no. 3) lightest solid element, a metal; used in lubricants and medicine

lithography method of printing in which parts of the printing plate are made greasy, so that greasy ink will stick to them

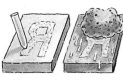

Draw image on plate with wax crayon... ...wet plate - water does not stick to wax... ...apply greasy ink, which sticks to wax but not wetted plate... ...press paper on to plate... ...finished print.

L

litmus dye used as an indicator: an acid turns it red, a base blue

logarithm power to which a base (usually 10) must be raised to give a certain number is the logarithm of the number; for example, $10^{0.22}$ is 1.6595869, so 0.22 is the logarithm of 1.6595869; using logarithms makes certain calculations easier

logarithmic scale scale used on graphs; at each division the number is ten times the previous one: 1, 10, 100 etc. (for an example see electromagnetic radiation)

logic circuit electric or electronic circuit in which certain inputs produce certain outputs according to logical rules (see gate); used in control systems

long wave a radio waveband (see electromagnetic radiation)

longitude position on the Earth's surface measured as an angle east or west of a line running north-south through Greenwich (the Greenwich meridian)

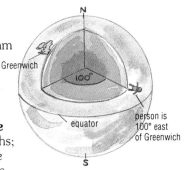

N
Greenwich
100°
equator
person is 100° east of Greenwich
S

lubrication reducing friction between two surfaces by separating them with a layer of fluid, such as oil or grease

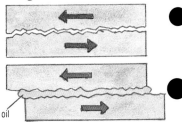

oil

luminescence
producing light by
a chemical reaction,
as a glow-worm does

lutetium (Lu, atomic
no. 71) element, a
metal

lymph clear fluid
in all parts of the
body, containing
lymphocytes (a type
of white blood
corpuscle); it helps
to fight infection

M

machine any device,
however simple, in
which a force applied
in one place has an
effect in another
place; for example a
lever, a ramp, a screw
thread, a wheel

machine tool
power-driven device
for shaping metal

Mach number speed
compared to speed of
sound: Mach 1 is
the speed of sound,
Mach 2 twice as fast

macro in front of
a word means 'long'
or 'large'

macromolecule very
large molecule, as in
a polymer

maglev magnetic
levitation: using
electromagnets to
lift a train above the
track so that it can
move without friction

magma molten rock
inside the Earth

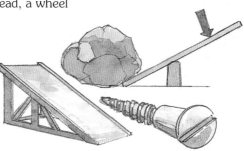

magnesium (Mg, atomic no. 12) element, a light metal; used to make light, strong alloys; burns with a brilliant white light, so is used in flashbulbs

magnet a permanent magnet is a piece of iron or similar material which has been magnetized; magnets have two different ends, called poles; unlike poles attract each other, like poles repel, but either pole will attract a piece of unmagnetized iron (see also electromagnet)

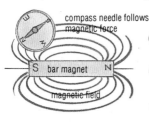

compass needle follows magnetic force

S bar magnet N

magnetic field

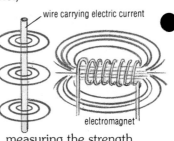

wire carrying electric current

electromagnet

magnetism force exerted by an object, caused by most of the electrons on its atoms spinning in the same direction, or by an electric current (this is also a movement of electrons)

magneto-hydro-dynamics (MHD) method of generating electricity from streams of hot plasma

magnetometer instrument for measuring the strength of magnetic fields

magnetron electronic device for producing microwaves; used in microwave ovens and radar

magnitude (of a star) measure of brightness: star of first magnitude is 2.51 times as bright as one of second magnitude

malleable able to be shaped by hammering; metals are malleable

mammal warm-blooded animal which feeds its young on milk

manganese (Mn, atomic no. 25) element, a pinkish metal; used in steel and alloys

manometer instrument for measuring pressure, using liquid in a U-shaped tube; one kind is used for measuring blood pressure

mantle layer of molten rock between the Earth's crust and core

marsupial animal which gives birth to young when they are very small and lets them go on growing in a pouch; for example kangaroo, opossum

mass amount of matter in an object; measured in kilograms, for example; when we say 'weight' we usually mean mass (see weight)

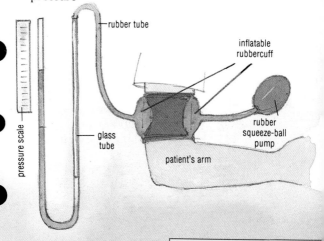

pressure scale

rubber tube

inflatable rubbercuff

rubber squeeze-ball pump

glass tube

patient's arm

mass-energy equation famous equation $E = mc^2$, which states how much energy is released when matter is turned into energy in a nuclear reaction; E is the energy in ergs (an erg is a ten millionth of a joule), m is the mass in grams, and c is the speed of light

mass spectroscopy separating heavy and light ions by firing them through a magnetic field; used as a means of chemical analysis

matrix framework in which something is set or built up

matter stuff things are made of

mechanical advantage ratio of load to effort in a machine

mechanics science dealing with matter and the forces on it

medium wave a radio waveband (see electromagnetic radiation)

mega- (M) in front of a word means 'a million'; for example megaton, a million tonnes

meiosis division of living cells to form gametes (sex cells); each new cell gets half a set of chromosomes

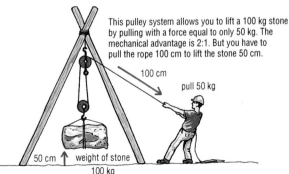

This pulley system allows you to lift a 100 kg stone by pulling with a force equal to only 50 kg. The mechanical advantage is 2:1. But you have to pull the rope 100 cm to lift the stone 50 cm.

100 cm

pull 50 kg

50 cm ↑ weight of stone 100 kg

membrane a thin sheet of any material

mendelevium (Md, atomic no. 101) element, a radioactive metal; not found in nature, made in a particle accelerator

meniscus curved edge of a liquid in a container; water and most liquids have a concave curve, mercury a convex one

concave meniscus

convex meniscus

mercury (Hg, atomic no. 80) element, the only metal that is a liquid at room temperature; used in electric switches and fluorescent tubes, batteries and explosives

meson particle consisting of two quarks

mesosphere layer of atmosphere from about 50 to 80 km above the Earth; this includes some of the ionosphere

metabolism series of chemical reactions happening in a living thing

metal any of a large group of elements, taking up most of the periodic table; all are shiny and conduct electricity

metal detector device for finding buried pieces of metal by the way in which they distort a magnetic field; even non-magnetic metals do this

metalloids a few elements which are on the borderline between metals and non-metals (see periodic table)

metamorphic of rocks: changed by heat and pressure inside the Earth; for example marble, which started as limestone

meteor small solid body from outer space which burns up in Earth's atmosphere before it reaches the ground

meteorite larger solid body from outer space which does not completely burn up, so that some of it hits the ground

meteorology science of the weather

metre (m) unit of length; originally supposed to be one ten millionth of the distance from the north pole to the equator, but they got the measurement slightly wrong

metric system system of measurement based on metres and grams rather than feet and pounds (for the scientific version, see MKS system)

methane (CH_4) hydrocarbon gas produced by rotting organic matter; for example natural gas and biogas

micro- (μ) in front of a word means 'very small' or 'one millionth'; for example microgram (μg), a millionth of a gram

microbe vague word for any single-celled living creature

microchip small piece of silicon or another semi-conductor formed into a tiny electronic circuit by 'doping' it with chemicals and etching tracks on the surface

micro-organism any very small living thing

micron micrometre (μm), a millionth of a metre

microscope device giving an enlarged image of small objects: a simple microscope is just a magnifying glass; a compound microscope has two lenses (see also electron microscope)

Compound Microscope - two lenses form a magnified image in reverse.

microtome cutter for making thin slices to look at under a microscope

microwaves electromagnetic radiation with wavelength from 1 to 300 mm

milli- (m) in front of a word means 'one thousandth'; for example millimetre, a thousandth of a metre

milling shaping metal by shaving pieces off it with a revolving cutter

mineral a useful material found in the earth, such as a metal ore; also used vaguely to mean a trace element

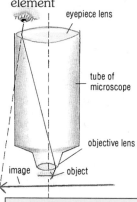

eyepiece lens

tube of microscope

objective lens

image   object

M

minute (') $\frac{1}{60}$ of an hour, or of a degree in angle measurement

mitosis normal method of division of living cells; each new cell gets a full set of chromosomes

mixture substance made of elements and/or compounds which are not linked to each other by bonds (see also compound)

MKS system official scientific system of measurement, where the basic units are the metre, the kilogram and the second, and other units are worked out from these; for example, a newton is the force required to give a mass of 1 kg an acceleration of 1 metre per second per second

mode state of something; one of the frequencies at which something tends to vibrate

model in science, any imitation of a real event used as a means of studying it

moderator substance used to slow down neutrons in a nuclear reactor; water, heavy water and graphite (carbon) are used

modulation putting information into a wave; for example adding a sound wave to a radio wave (see amplitude modulation, frequency modulation)

moiré stripy pattern caused by interference between two grid patterns

mole (mol) amount of a substance which contains as many atoms (or molecules, if it has molecules) as there are atoms in 12 g of carbon; used to measure the concentration of a solution; a 'molar' solution has one mole per litre

molecule group of atoms, either of a pure element or a compound: oxygen exists in molecules of two atoms (O_2); water has molecules of two hydrogen and one oxygen atom (H_2O)

mollusc type of animal with no backbone and often a shell; includes oyster, squid, snail

molybdenum (Mo, atomic no. 42) element, a metal; used in alloys; molybdenum disulphide (MoS_2) is a lubricant added to oils

momentum mass of a moving object multiplied by its speed; linear momentum (in a straight line) and angular momentum (of a revolving body) can be measured

mon(o)- in front of a word means 'single'

monochromatic having a single colour

mordant chemical used to make a dye stick to a fabric

morphology science of the shape of living things

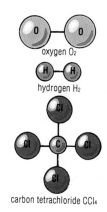

oxygen O_2

hydrogen H_2

carbon tetrachloride CCl_4

M

motion laws of (1) everything keeps moving in a straight line at a steady speed (or stays still) unless a force acts on it; (2) any change depends on the size of the force, and happens in the direction in which the force acts; (3) every action produces an equal and opposite reaction (see reaction)

mutation sudden change in DNA, producing a new kind of offspring

N

nadir point in the sky on the opposite side of the Earth from you

nadir

nano- (n) in front of a word means 'one thousand millionth'; for example nanometre (nm), a thousand millionth of a metre

natural frequency rate at which something vibrates when struck; for example a bell which sounds a certain note

natural gas gas found with oil deposits, mainly methane; used as a fuel

negative (electricity) having more electrons than normal (an electron carries a negative charge); the negative terminal of a battery is the one the electrons come out of

negative (mathematics) of a number: less than 0

nematode type of small animal, for example a flatworm; many are parasites

neodymium (Nd, atomic no. 60) element, a metal; used in lasers

neon (Ne, atomic no. 10) element, an inert gas; used in fluorescent tubes (real neon lights are red; others use argon and coloured glass)

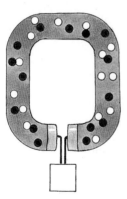

neptunium (Np, atomic no. 93) element, a radioactive metal; not found in nature, made in a particle accelerator

nerve 'wiring system' of the body, carrying electrical messages to and from the brain

neural network computer system which imitates structure of brain, and can learn in the same way

neuron nerve cell

neutral (chemistry) neither acid nor basic

neutralization reaction between acid and base to produce salt and water

newton unit of force; roughly the weight on Earth of an object with a mass of 100 g

niche role in an ecosystem; if a creature filling a niche becomes extinct, usually another creature evolves to fill it

nickel (Ni, atomic no. 28) element, a metal; used in alloys ('silver' coins) and for plating steel

niobium (Nb, atomic no. 41) element, a metal; used in heat-resistant alloys

nitrate compound of a metal, nitrogen and oxygen; for example saltpetre (potassium nitrate, KNO_3)

nitric acid (HNO_3) strong acid; used to make fertilisers, explosives etc.

nitrogen (N, atomic no. 7) element, a gas which makes up 78% of the atmosphere; liquid nitrogen at -195°C is used to keep things very cold; its compounds are vital to plants and the most important part of fertilisers

nobelium (No, atomic no. 102) element, a radioactive metal; not found in nature, made in a particle accelerator

noble gases another name for the inert gases, because they almost never react with other elements (see noble metals)

noble metals group of metals (see periodic table) named because they seldom react with other elements, so they do not rust or tarnish; opposite of base metals

node point in a standing wave where there is least movement

noise (electronics) unwanted random waves added to a signal

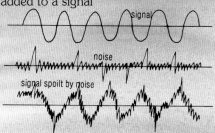

non-metals group of elements in the top right-hand corner of the periodic table, named simply because most of the table consists of metals

normal (chemistry) of a solution: molar (see mole)

normal (mathematics) line at right angles to a surface

nuclear physics science of events in the nucleus of atoms

nucleus (biology; plural nuclei) central part of a cell, which contains most of its DNA

nucleus (atomic; plural nuclei) central part of an atom; it consists of protons and (except in hydrogen) neutrons

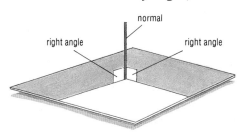

O

objective lens lens at the opposite end of a telescope or microscope from your eye

obtuse of an angle: greater than 90°

oceanography science of oceans and seas

octane (C_8H_{18}) a hydrocarbon; the quality of petrol is rated by comparing it with octane: '100 octane' means that it performs as well as pure octane

octave a note one octave higher than another note has twice the frequency

oesophagus tube through which food goes from the mouth to the stomach

ohm (Ω) unit of electrical resistance

oil liquid greasy substance; some plants contain vegetable oils; petroleum is another kind of oil (see also fat)

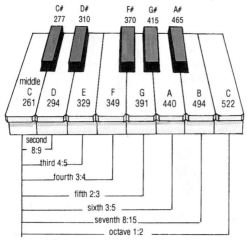

Octave: the frequencies (in hertz) of the notes in one octave on a piano, and the ratios between them. The simplest ratios, with the lowest numbers, sound most pleasant when the two notes are played together - a fifth (2:3) sounds better than a seventh (8:15).

O

omnivore animal that eats both meat and plants

opaque not letting light (or some other radiation) through

optics science of light

orbit path taken by a satellite, for example the Moon around the Earth: it is held in orbit by the balance between the Earth's gravity and centrifugal force

ore mineral from which a metal can be extracted

organic chemistry science of organic compounds

organic compounds all compounds of carbon except for a few very simple ones; carbon compounds are the basis of all living things

oscillation regular vibration

oscilloscope device for showing electrical oscillations on a screen

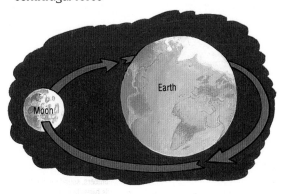

O

osmium (Os, atomic no. 76) heaviest element, a metal similar to platinum; used in alloys with platinum

osmosis flow of liquid between two solutions on either side of a semi-permeable membrane; it flows to the side where the solution is more concentrated

ovary part of a female animal which produces eggs, or of a plant which produces ovules

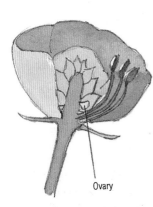
Ovary

oviparous egg-laying

ovule female sex cell of a plant

ovum egg

oxidation adding oxygen to a compound (or sometimes just making its atoms lose electrons); when one substance is oxidized, another is reduced (see reduction); burning is very fast oxidation, rusting is slower; animals get energy from food by oxidizing it, which is why they need to breathe in oxygen

oxide compound of an element with oxygen; for example zinc oxide (ZnO)

oxygen (O, atomic no. 8) element, a gas which makes up 21% of the air; vital to animals which breathe it, and also to allow things to burn (see oxidation)

ozone form of oxygen with a molecule made of three oxygen atoms (O_3); a layer of ozone in the upper atmosphere, 1530 km above the Earth, shields the surface from harmful ultra-violet radiation

P

pacemaker device which sends pulses of electricity into the heart to keep it beating steadily

palaeontology science of life in ancient times

palladium (Pd, atomic no. 46) element, a metal similar to platinum; used as a catalyst in margarine manufacture

parabola curved path of an object when it is thrown; or any line of this shape

parallel side by side; two parallel lines never meet, no matter how far you extend them; two electrical components mounted side by side in a circuit are also said to be in parallel

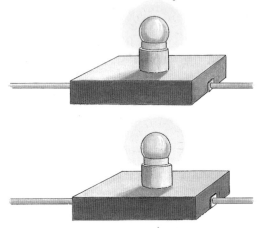

parameter (mathematics) variable kept constant so that other variables can be studied

parasite creature living in or on another, from which it gets its food

parthenogenesis reproducing without sex

particle (physics) one of the pieces of which an atom is made (proton, neutron and electron); there are also many other kinds of particle (for example the photon)

pascal (Pa) unit of pressure; 1 newton per square metre

pasteurize to heat a foodstuff (without actually boiling it), killing most bacteria in it, so that it keeps longer

pathogenic causing disease

pendulum weight swinging on a string or rod; the rate at which it swings depends entirely on the length

penumbra region of half shadow when something is lit by a large object, such as the Sun

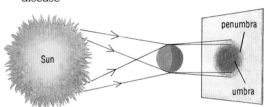

perigee innermost point of a satellite's orbit around the Earth

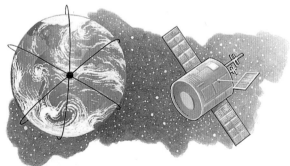

period time taken for one full cycle of a repeated action, for example one swing of a pendulum

periodic table a way of listing the elements by writing them in rows in the order of their atomic numbers; the rows can be arranged so that elements which are alike form groups; elements of a particular kind come up at regular intervals along the rows

Symbols for Elements

Ac	actinium	**He**	helium	**Rh**	rhodium
		Hf	hafnium	**Rn**	radon
Ag	silver	**Hg**	mercury	**Ru**	ruthenium
Al	aluminium	**Ho**	holmium	**S**	sulphur
Am	americum	**I**	iodine	**Sb**	antimony
Ar	argon	**In**	indium	**Sc**	scandium
As	arsenic	**Ir**	iridium	**Se**	selenium
At	astatine	**K**	potassium	**Si**	silicon
Au	gold	**Kr**	krypton	**Sm**	samarium
B	boron	**La**	lanthanum	**Sn**	tin
Ba	barium	**Li**	lithium	**Sr**	strontium
Be	beryllium	**Lu**	lutetium	**Ta**	tantalum
Bi	bismuth	**Lw**	lawrencium	**Tb**	terbium
Bk	berkelium	**Md**	mendelevium	**Tc**	technetium
Br	bromine	**Mg**	magnesium	**Te**	tellurium
C	carbon	**Mn**	manganese	**Th**	thorium
Ca	calcium	**Mo**	molybdenum	**Ti**	titanium
Cd	cadmium	**N**	nitrogen	**Tl**	thallium
Ce	cerium	**Na**	sodium	**Tm**	thulium
Cf	californium	**Nb**	niobium	**U**	uranium
Cl	chlorine	**Nd**	neodymium	**Une**	unnilennium
Cm	curium	**Ne**	neon	**Unh**	unnilhexium
Co	cobalt	**Ni**	nickel	**Unp**	unnilpentium*
Cr	chromium	**No**	nobelium	**Unq**	unnilquadium†
Cs	caesium	**Np**	neptunium	**Uns**	unnilseptium
Cu	copper	**O**	oxygen	**V**	vanadium
Dy	dysprosium	**Os**	osmium	**W**	tungsten
Er	erbium	**P**	phosphorus	**Xe**	xenon
Es	einsteinium	**Pa**	protactinium	**Y**	yttrium
Eu	europium	**Pb**	lead	**Yb**	ytterbium
F	fluorine	**Pd**	palladium	**Z**	zinc
Fe	iron	**Pm**	promethium	**Zr**	zirconium
Fm	fermium	**Po**	polonium		
Fr	francium	**Pr**	praseodymium		
Ga	gallium	**Pt**	platinum		
Gd	gadolinium	**Pu**	plutonium		
Ge	germanium	**Ra**	radium		
H	hydrogen	**Rb**	rubidium		
		Re	rhenium		

* also known as hahnium (Ha) or nielsbohrium

† also known as kurchatovium (Ku) or rutherfordium (Rf)

Periodic Table of the Elements

Key for each element:

atomic number	89
atomic symbol	**Ac**
atomic weight (parentheses indicate most stable isotope)	(227)

KEY

- Alkali Metals
- Alkaline Earth Metals
- Rare Earth Elements
- Actinides
- Transition Metals
- Platinum Metals
- Noble Metals
- Metalloids
- Halogens
- Inert Gases
- Non-Metals

Main Table

1	2	3	4	5	6	7	8	9	10	11	12	13	14	15	16	17	18
1 **H** 1.00794																	2 **He** 4.00260
3 **Li** 6.941	4 **Be** 9.01218											5 **B** 10.81	6 **C** 12.011	7 **N** 14.0067	8 **O** 15.9994	9 **F** 18.998403	10 **Ne** 20.179
11 **Na** 22.98977	12 **Mg** 24.305											13 **Al** 26.98154	14 **Si** 28.0855	15 **P** 30.97376	16 **S** 32.06	17 **Cl** 35.453	18 **Ar** 39.948
19 **K** 39.0983	20 **Ca** 40.08	21 **Sc** 44.9559	22 **Ti** 47.88	23 **V** 50.9415	24 **Cr** 51.996	25 **Mn** 54.9380	26 **Fe** 55.847	27 **Co** 58.9332	28 **Ni** 58.69	29 **Cu** 63.546	30 **Zn** 65.38	31 **Ga** 69.72	32 **Ge** 72.59	33 **As** 74.9216	34 **Se** 78.96	35 **Br** 79.904	36 **Kr** 83.80
37 **Rb** 85.4678	38 **Sr** 87.62	39 **Y** 88.9059	40 **Zr** 91.22	41 **Nb** 92.9064	42 **Mo** 95.94	43 **Tc** (98)	44 **Ru** 101.07	45 **Rh** 102.9055	46 **Pd** 106.42	47 **Ag** 107.8682	48 **Cd** 112.41	49 **In** 114.82	50 **Sn** 118.69	51 **Sb** 121.75	52 **Te** 127.60	53 **I** 126.9045	54 **Xe** 131.29
55 **Cs** 132.9054	56 **Ba** 137.33	57 **La** 138.9055	72 **Hf** 178.49	73 **Ta** 180.7479*	74 **W** 183.85	75 **Re** 186.207	76 **Os** 190.2	77 **Ir** 192.2	78 **Pt** 195.08	79 **Au** 196.9665	80 **Hg** 200.59*	81 **Tl** 204.383	82 **Pb** 207.2	83 **Bi** 208.9804	84 **Po** (209)	85 **At** (210)	86 **Rn** (222)
87 **Fr** (223)	88 **Ra** 226.0254	89 **Ac** (227)	104 **Unq†** (261)	105 **Unp*** (262)	106 **Unh** (263)	107 **Uns** (262)		109 **Une** (266)									

Lanthanide series (Rare Earth Elements)

57 **La** 138.9055	58 **Ce** 140.12	59 **Pr** 140.9077	60 **Nd** 144.24	61 **Pm** (145)	62 **Sm** 150.36	63 **Eu** 151.96	64 **Gd** 157.25	65 **Tb** 158.9254	66 **Dy** 162.50	67 **Ho** 164.9304	68 **Er** 167.26	69 **Tm** 168.9342	70 **Yb** 173.04	71 **Lu** 174.967

Actinide series (Radioactive Rare Earth Elements)

89 **Ac** 227.0278	90 **Th** 232.0381	91 **Pa** 231.0359	92 **U** 238.0289	93 **Np** 237.0482	94 **Pu** (244)	95 **Am** (243)	96 **Cm** (247)	97 **Bk** (247)	98 **Cf** (252)	99 **Es** (254)	100 **Fm** (257)	101 **Md** (258)	102 **No** (259)	103 **Lr** (260)

† Other proposed names are kurchatovium (USSR) and rutherfordium (US).

* Other proposed names are nielsbohrium (USSR) and hahnium (US).

periscope device with two mirrors or prisms for looking over the top of something

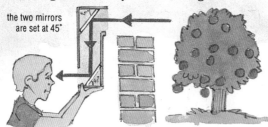

the two mirrors are set at 45°

permeable allowing something to pass through

perpendicular at right angles

pesticide substance for killing pests

petroleum oil found in the ground; formed over millions of years from the remains of living things; used to make fuel and many chemicals

pewter alloy of tin and antimony (old pewter also contains lead)

pH value measure of acidity or alkalinity; pH 0 is highly acid, pH 7 is neutral, pH 14 is highly alkaline

phase state of matter (solid, liquid or gas); or one part of a colloid or suspension; or stage of wave motion (two waves are in phase if their peaks are in the same place)

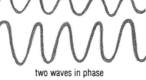

two waves in phase

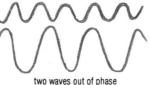

two waves out of phase

phosphate compound of a metal, phosphorus and oxygen; for example sodium phosphate (Na_3PO_4)

phosphorescence
glow similar to
fluorescence except
that it continues
after the radiation
has been absorbed

phosphorus
(P, atomic no. 15)
element, a non-metal;
used to make fertilisers
and matches (see
also bone)

photoelectric cell
device which absorbs
energy from light and
gives it out as an
electric current; many
uses, such as light
meters for cameras
(see solar cell)

**photoengraving and
photolithography**
printing methods in
which a plate is coated
with a light-sensitive
substance, the image
is photographed on
to it, and it is treated
with chemicals to
make a printing plate

photomicrograph
photograph taken
through a microscope

photon particle
that carries
electromagnetic
radiation

photosynthesis
process by which
plants take in carbon
dioxide from the air
and turn it into carbon
compounds, which
they use, and oxygen,
which they release;
sunlight provides
energy to drive the
reaction, and
chlorophyll acts as a
catalyst; this reaction
renews the oxygen
in the air which is
used up by animals
breathing and
by burning

CO_2

O

P

physics science of matter and energy

pi (π) ratio of circumference of a circle to diameter of a circle: 3.1415926535 8979323846... etc.

pipette thin glass tube with wide part in middle, used for sucking up a small amount of liquid

pitch frequency; for example of a musical note, or of the ridges of a screw thread

plane (mathematics) flat surface

plankton small plants and animals which drift in the sea

plasma (biology) liquid part of blood, in which the cells float

plasma (physics) ionized gas

plastics organic polymers formed as a soft substance and moulded to shape; some are synthetic (polystyrene, made from oil), some made by altering natural substances (celluloid, made from cellulose), some natural (shellac, made by an insect)

plate tectonics study of the movement of the huge slabs which make up the Earth's crust

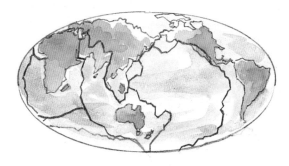

platinum (Pt, atomic no. 78) element, a bright metal which does not corrode and resists most chemicals; used in jewellery and scientific instruments and as a catalyst

platinum metals group of elements including platinum, all very similar (see periodic table)

plutonium (Pu, atomic no. 94) element, a radioactive metal; uncommon in nature and mostly produced in nuclear reactors; very poisonous

pneumatic powered by compressed air

polarity having opposite ends, such as north and south poles of a magnet, or positive and negative terminals of a battery

P

polarization vibration of waves, such as light or radio waves, in a particular direction (up and down or from side to side)

Light may vibrate in any direction

... but a polarizing filter such as a Polaroid sunglass lens only lets through those that are vibrating in one direction

pole one of the two ends of a magnet, called 'north' or 'south' because the north pole of a magnetic compass needle points to the north pole of the Earth (which is actually a south magnetic pole, see compass)

pollen male sex cell of a plant

polonium (Po, atomic no. 84) element, a radioactive metal

poly- in front of a word means 'many'; often used in names of plastics such as polystyrene or fibres such as polyamide (nylon), which are polymers

polymer substance in which many molecules are joined to make long chains; such substances can be very strong; for example cellulose, plastics

positive (electricity) having fewer electrons than normal; the negative terminal of a battery is the one the electrons pass into

positive (mathematics) of a number: greater than 0

potassium (K, atomic no. 19) element, a light metal; many compounds used in the chemical industry; potash (potassium carbonate, K_2CO_3) is used in fertilisers

potential energy energy that exists in the position of an object: when you lift a book from the floor to a table you add potential energy to it; if the book falls off the table this is turned to kinetic energy

power (mathematics) number of times a quantity is multiplied or divided together: 64 is 4 x 4 x 4, that is 4 to the power of 3, written 4^3

praseodymium (Pr, atomic no. 59) element, a metal

precipitate to come out of solution as a solid; a substance which has done this

predator animal that eats other animals

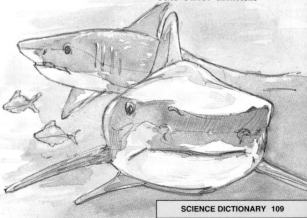

pressure force acting on a given area; the pressure of the atmosphere at sea level is 100 kPa (kilopascals)

projectile something thrown or fired, such as a ball or a bullet

primate type of animal: includes lemurs, monkeys, apes and people

protactinium (Pa, atomic no. 91) element, a radioactive metal

protein main substance of which animals are made, also found in plants; has long molecules composed of amino acids

protist single-celled creature; group includes protozoa but not bacteria or algae

promethium (Pm, atomic no. 61) element, a radioactive metal; not found in nature, made in a particle accelerator

protozoan single-celled animal

quadrat sample of ground 1 metre square, used in surveys

quadruped animal with four feet

qualitative dealing with kind or type, without giving an exact measurement

quantitative dealing with amount

quantum (plural quanta) smallest possible unit; a photon is a quantum of light

quantum mechanics science explaining small-scale events in terms of quanta

quark smallest object yet discovered, one of the pieces of which atomic particles are made; a baryon (such as a proton) is made of three quarks, and a meson of two

quartz watch watch in which time is kept by the vibration of a crystal of quartz (silicon dioxide, SiO_2)

radar system for 'seeing' objects by sending out radio waves

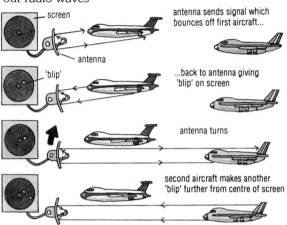

screen
antenna

'blip'

antenna turns

antenna sends signal which bounces off first aircraft...

...back to antenna giving 'blip' on screen

second aircraft makes another 'blip' further from centre of screen

radial symmetry
having the same shape when seen from several points around a circle, as in a spoked wheel or a starfish

radian (rad)
measurement of angle, based on line drawn around edge of a circle, equal in length to radius of circle

radical (chemistry)
group of atoms which usually stay together during reactions; for example the carboxyl group (-COOH)

radiocarbon dating
method of finding age of anything that was once alive by measuring how much of a radioisotope of carbon (carbon-14) in it has decayed to nitrogen

radius line from centre to edge of circle

radiation stream of waves or particles (see alpha, beta, gamma, electromagnetic radiation)

radioactivity giving off radiation by unstable elements (see isotope)

radioisotope see isotope

radiotelescope device for picking up radio waves from objects in outer space

radium (Ra, atomic no. 88) element, a radioactive metal; radium 'needles' are put into cancers to kill them

radon (Rn, atomic no. 86) element, a heavy radioactive gas produced by the decay of uranium; in some regions it seeps out of rocks into the basements of houses and is thought to cause lung disease

ram hydraulic piston used to provide a push; for example to lift the body of a tipper truck

rare earth elements group of metals (see periodic table), named because they are found mainly in some rare ores; all are similar to aluminium

ratio relationship of two quantities; if one is twice the other, the ratio is 2:1

reaction (chemistry) event in which atoms of two or more elements bond together to make compounds or split apart to destroy compounds; this involves only the electrons on the outside of the atoms

reaction (nuclear) see fission, fusion

reaction (physics) when force is applied to an object, this is resisted by an equal reaction force in the opposite direction; when you push a car, the reaction force makes it hard to move the car

reactor (nuclear) device in which nuclear fission produces heat; various types, including pressurized water (see picture) and fast breeder, which makes plutonium that can be used as fuel in another reactor; scientists are trying to build a fusion reactor, which would be more powerful, safer and cleaner

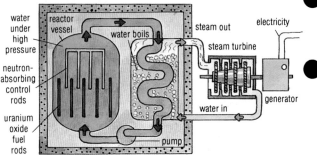

reciprocal of a number: 1 divided by that number; the reciprocal of 0.5 is $1/0.5$, that is 2; and the reciprocal of 2 is $1/2$ or 0.5

rectifier electrical device for converting alternating current to direct current

red blood cell cell in blood which carries oxygen around the body; the red colour is due to iron

red shift difference in colour of an object when it is approaching or going away; stars that are moving rapidly away from Earth look redder than they really are; an example of the Doppler effect

reduction removing oxygen from a compound (or sometimes just adding electrons to its atoms); when one substance is reduced another is always oxidized (see oxidation)

reflection 'bouncing' of light or other radiation off a surface; if it strikes a flat surface at a certain angle, it is reflected at the opposite angle

refraction change in the direction of light when it passes from one transparent substance to another

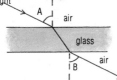

refractory heatproof

relativity two complex theories: general relativity states that nothing can travel faster than light and tries to explain the strange results of this; special relativity states that gravitation bends light rays

relay electrical switch moved by sending a small current through an electromagnet

reptile type of cold-blooded, scaly animal: lizards, snakes, crocodiles, dinosaurs etc.

resin type of polymer, including plastics, adhesives and paints

resistance (electrical) unwillingness of a material to let electric current pass through it

resistor electrical device providing resistance

resolution ability of (for example) a camera to show very small objects

resonance strong vibration caused when an object is made to vibrate at its natural frequency

retort vessel used for distillation

R

rhenium (Re, atomic no. 75) element, a metal; used in scientific instruments

rhodium (Rh, atomic no. 45) element, a metal similar to platinum; used to plate metals, in catalysts and in alloys

RNA (ribonucleic acid) substance in cells of living things, shaped like one side of a strand of DNA; carries information from DNA and uses it to make proteins; some viruses use RNA instead of DNA as an information store

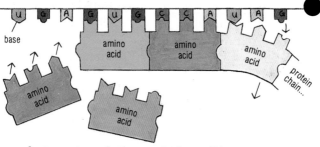

rocket engine which works by sending out a stream of hot gas but, unlike a jet engine, carries its own supply of oxygen so that it can work in space

root number which, when multiplied by itself, produces a given number: the square root of 9 is 3 (3 x 3 = 9); the cube root of 64 is 4 (4 x 4 x 4 = 64)

rubidium (Rb, atomic no. 37) element, a slightly radioactive metal; explodes when it touches water

ruminant animal which chews the cud - brings up food it has already swallowed and chews it again - and has several stomachs, so that it can digest grass efficiently; for example a cow

ruthenium (Ru, atomic no. 44) element, a metal similar to platinum; used in alloys with platinum

rutherfordium (Rf, atomic no. 104; also called kurchatovium, Ku) element, a radioactive metal; not found in nature, made in a particle accelerator

S

salt compound which can be formed when hydrogen atoms in an acid are replaced with atoms of a metal, for example table salt (sodium chloride, NaCl) from sodium (Na) and hydrochloric acid (HCl) or from a reaction between an acid and a base such as hydrochloric acid and caustic soda: $HCl + NaOH > NaCl + H_2O$

saltpetre potassium nitrate (KNO_3); used in gunpowder

samarium (Sm, atomic no. 62) element, a slightly radioactive metal

saprophyte plant or fungus that lives on rotting remains

satellite something in orbit around a planet (usually); the Moon is a satellite of the Earth

saturation highest possible level; a saturated solution contains the largest amount that will dissolve

scan to move back and forth across an image, recording it a strip at a time, as a television camera does

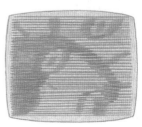

scandium (Sc, atomic no. 21) element, a metal

second (") $\frac{1}{3600}$ of an hour, or of a degree in angle measurement

secretion sending a substance (such as a hormone) out of a cell

sedimentary of rock: formed from sediment falling on to the sea floor; for example limestone

segment part of circle shaped like slice of cake; or one section of an animal such as a worm

selenium (Se, atomic no. 34) element, a non-metal; used in photoelectric cells

semiconductor material which conducts electricity to some extent; these materials are important in electronics, where they are used to make transistors, microchips etc.

semi-permeable of a membrane: allowing small molecules through, but not big ones

series of electrical components: placed end to end in a circuit

servo machinery for moving something in a controlled way; for example the power steering system of a car

sex cell a cell used to make offspring; for example, a sperm or egg; it has only half the chromosomes of a normal (somatic) cell, so that when two sex cells fuse, the offspring gets a full set

sex chromosome an X- or Y-shaped chromosome which determines the sex of offspring; in mammals the mother always supplies an X, the father an X or a Y; if the offspring gets XX it will be female, if XY, male

sex linkage of a gene: being on the X chromosome; if a male inherits an X chromosome carrying a disease he will suffer from the disease; if a female inherits it, her other good X chromosome will keep her well but she may pass the bad gene on to her children

X = good X chromosome

X = bad X chromosome

normal carrier
father mother

sperm   egg

XY   normal son

XY   son with disease

normal daughter

carrier daughter

sextant a sixth of a circle; a navigation instrument in this shape, used to measure the angle of the Sun above the horizon

shear stress applied to something in the same plane as one of its flat surfaces, so that if it breaks, the broken piece will slide along

shock wave wave of highly compressed air sent out by an explosion or a supersonic aircraft

short circuit connection across an electrical circuit which allows the current to take a short cut

short wave a radio waveband (see electromagnetic radiation)

shutter device for letting light into a camera

SI (Système Internationale d'Unités) internationally agreed system of metric measurements

sidereal to do with the stars; a sidereal day is the time the Earth takes to turn once in relation to the stars (23 hours 56 minutes)

sign (mathematics) plus or minus

signal something that carries information; for example a radio signal

silicon (Si, atomic no. 14) element, a non-metal and a semiconductor; used to make microchips and photoelectric cells

silicone a polymer containing silicon and a hydrocarbon; types include plastics, synthetic rubbers and gels

silver (Ag, atomic no. 47) element, a shiny metal, very easy to shape, conducts electricity best of all metals; used in ornaments, electronics, and to make chemicals in photographic film

sine see trigonometry

sine wave wave which rises and falls smoothly; the shape can be drawn as a graph of the sine of an increasing number

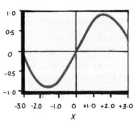

sin x

sinus hollow in bone of skull to make it lighter

slag stony waste product from metal smelting

slide rule device for quick, rough calculations: two rulers marked with logarithmic scales and sliding against each other

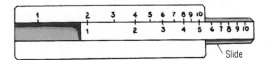

Slide

smelt to extract metal from an ore by heating it

soda various sodium compounds: caustic soda (sodium hydroxide, NaOH), washing soda (sodium carbonate, $Na_2CO_3.10H_2O$), bicarbonate of soda (sodium hydrogen carbonate, $NaHCO_3$)

sodium (Na, atomic no. 11) element, a light metal with a low melting point; molten sodium is used in nuclear reactors to carry away heat

solar cell large photoelectric cell made of silicon,

producing useful amounts of electricity; used, for example, for telephones in remote places

solder to join two pieces of metal with molten metal; or the metal used for this; often an alloy of lead and tin

solenoid wire coil acting as an electromagnet

solid substance which has a definite shape and size

solid state of an electronic circuit: using semiconductors, as opposed to valves filled with gas

solute something dissolved in a liquid

solution a completely smooth liquid mixture; it can consist of a solid, liquid or gas dissolved in a liquid

solvent liquid in which something dissolves

somatic cell a normal body cell, as opposed to a sex cell

sonar another name for echo sounding

sound wave motion in the air caused by moving objects; the waves consist of regions of different air pressure

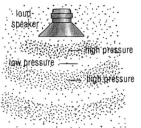

sound, speed of 1225 km/h at sea level, and slower with increasing height

space-time idea that time is a dimension like length, breadth or height, so that the Universe has four dimensions

spark (electric) electrons jumping through the air or a gas

species a group of living things which are closely enough related to breed with each other and produce offspring of the same kind (some species can interbreed to produce hybrids)

specific gravity old name for density

specific heat amount of heat needed to raise temperature of 1 g of a substance by 1°C

spectrograph instrument for looking at a spectrum

spectrum range of wavelengths of any kind of radiation; the spectrum of visible light is all the colours of the rainbow, but you can also talk about the spectrum of radio or sound waves

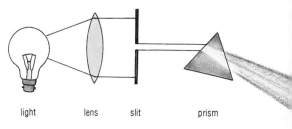

light   lens   slit   prism

sperm sex cells of a male animal

spin of a particle: some particles, such as electrons, spin constantly; if most of these spin the same way it causes magnetism

spinal cord bundle of nerves running down back; main path of nerves from brain to rest of body

spirit old term for anything distilled; now mainly means alcohol

spore tiny 'seed' of a simple plant, fungus, bacterium etc.

square (mathematics) number multiplied by itself once

stabilizer something which slows down a chemical reaction, the opposite of a catalyst; stabilizers are added to foods to make them keep longer

stable of an element: not likely to decompose and therefore not radioactive

stainless steel alloy steel containing chromium, and usually nickel

S

standing wave wave which goes from side to side but does not move along; for example, the vibration of a guitar string

starch carbohydrate made by plants as a food store; for example, a potato is mostly starch

stamen male part of a flower, which produces pollen

state of matter: see phase

static electricity electric charge, as opposed to current: the electricity does not flow

statics science of stationary objects and the forces acting on them

statistics branch of mathematics dealing with observed facts and making predictions from them

steam water in gas state, above boiling point; below this temperature it is water vapour

steel iron with a small amount of carbon added, which makes it much tougher

stereo- in front of a word means 'broad' or 'solid'; for example stereophonic sound, which seems to come from a wide area

stereoscopic seeing things in 3D; each eye sees the scene from a different viewpoint, and the brain uses the difference between the images to give a sense of depth

sterile unable to breed; or free of bacteria and other 'germs'

sterilize to kill bacteria by heating at least to boiling point

stethoscope device for listening to the heart or chest: a small diaphragm picks up the sound and sends it along tubes to the ears

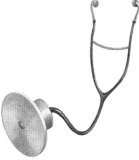

stigma female part of a flower, which picks up pollen

still device for distilling liquids

STOL short take-off and landing

stop (photography)

same as f number

stimulus event which makes a living thing react; it might be a noise, a smell, a change in temperature, etc.

stratosphere layer of atmosphere from roughly 15 to 50 km above the Earth; air here is thin and cold

storage battery accumulator

strain change in shape of an object when there is a stress on it; for example, bending a spring

stratum (plural strata) a layer; for example of rock

stress force acting on a certain area of an object; usually measured in pascals: this is the same as pressure, but the word 'stress' is used for force acting in a particular direction (see shear, torque)

stroboscope flashing light which can be used, for example, to look at a spinning wheel by lighting it only when it is in a certain position

strontium (Sr, atomic no. 38) element, a metal; used in fireworks to give a red colour; the radioactive isotope strontium-90, created by nuclear bombs, is dangerous because the body mistakes it for calcium and it gets into bones

subatomic smaller than an atom; an atom is made of subatomic particles

sucrose see sugar

sugar one of many types of carbohydrate: ordinary white sugar is sucrose ($C_{12}H_{22}O_{11}$), which can be split into glucose and fructose

sulphate compound of a metal, sulphur and oxygen; for example copper sulphate, $CuSO_4$

sulphur (S, atomic no. 16) element, a non-metal with three allotropes; much used in the chemical industry, for example to make sulphuric acid

sulphuric acid (H_2SO_4) strong acid; used in accumulators, and to make many chemicals, including dyes, explosives, fertilisers, detergents and rayon

sunspot storm on surface of the Sun (other stars have them too), with a strong magnetic field which can affect the Earth, causing the aurora borealis and radio interference

superconductivity ability of some materials to conduct electricity without any resistance when they are cooled to very low temperatures

supercooling cooling a liquid to below its normal freezing point without it freezing in the normal way; this may be done by cooling it so fast that there is no time for crystals to form; glass is a material of this kind

superheating strictly, heating a liquid above its boiling point without it boiling; but mostly used to refer to steam which has been heated above the temperature of boiling water, for example to drive a steam turbine

supersonic travelling faster than the speed of sound (see hypersonic)

surface tension tendency of the surface of a liquid to pull itself tight, so that it has a smooth shape (see diagram below)

SURFACE TENSION   surface of liquid

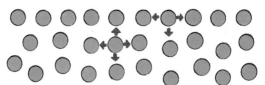

surfactant a substance that affects surface tension; for example, a detergent, which uses this effect to pull the dirt out of fabrics

surge sudden rise in voltage in an electrical device, which often happens for a moment after it is switched on, and may blow its fuse

suspension small solid specks hanging in a liquid; for example muddy water

symbiosis two living things existing together, to the advantage of both of them; an example is a lichen

synapse electrical connection between two nerve cells; learning and memory are processes in which synapses are strengthened

synthesize to build up from simpler materials; a synthesizer is a musical instrument which builds up sounds by adding simple wave forms together

synthetic made from simpler materials: nylon is a synthetic fibre because it is made from simple compounds, but rayon, which is made from the complex material cellulose, is not

tachometer instrument measuring rate at which something spins

tangent a line touching the edge of a circle; or a trigonometrical ratio (see trigonometry)

tantalum (Ta, atomic no. 73) element, a metal; used in the chemical industry as a corrosion-resistant coating

tape recording recording a signal in the form of magnetic areas on a plastic tape coated with iron oxide or chromium dioxide, both of which can be magnetized

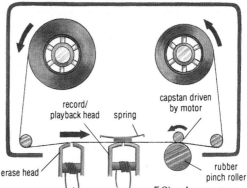

record/playback head   spring   capstan driven by motor

erase head   rubber pinch roller

taxonomy science of classifying living things into groups and finding relationships between them

technetium (Tc, atomic no. 43) element, a radioactive metal; not found in nature, made in a particle accelerator

tele- in front of a word means 'distant'

telescope device for giving a larger image of distant objects

tellurium (Te, atomic no. 52) element, a metal; alloyed with lead to strengthen it

temper heat metal and cool it quickly, changing the crystal structure and making the metal harder

temperature how hot something is but not the amount of heat energy in it, which depends on both its temperature and its size

tendon strong band of collagen attaching a muscle to a bone

terbium (Tb, atomic no. 65) element, a metal

terminal velocity maximum downward speed a falling object can reach: this depends on its mass and its air resistance

testis (plural testes) organ of a male animal which produces sperm

thallium (Tl, atomic no. 81) element, a metal; compounds are very poisonous

theodolite instrument for measuring angles accurately when surveying land: a small telescope pivoted on a scale of degrees

theorem statement logically proved to be true

therm unit of heat used by fuel companies: 100,000 kilojoules

thermo- in front of a word means 'to do with heat'

thermodynamics science of heat and energy

thermometer instrument for measuring temperature

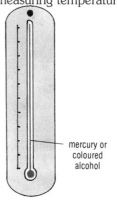

mercury or coloured alcohol

thermoplastic type of plastic which can be melted

thermosetting type of plastic which will burn rather than melt

thermosphere layer of the atmosphere from about 80 to 650 km above the Earth; there is very little air, but what there is is heated to a high temperature by the Sun

thermostat device for controlling temperature; for example, to keep a room at about 20°C, it will switch on the heating when the temperature falls to 18°C and switch it off when it rises to 22°C

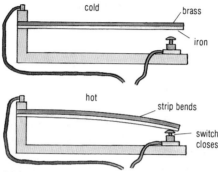

cold

brass

iron

hot

strip bends

switch closes

thixotropic of a solid: turning to a liquid when disturbed; for example quicksand

thorax chest of an animal; middle section of an insect, to which the legs are attached

thorium (Th, atomic no. 90) element, a radioactive metal; used as a fuel in some nuclear reactors

threshold level at which something begins to happen; for example, the brightness that a

light must reach before we can see it

thrust pushing force produced by a rocket or jet engine

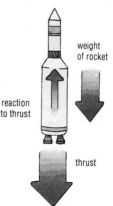

weight of rocket

reaction to thrust

thrust

thulium (Tm, atomic no. 69) element, a metal; has a radioisotope used as a source of X-rays

tin (Sn, atomic no. 50) element, a metal; used as a rust-resistant coating for steel, and alloyed with lead to make solder

tissue stuff of which plants and animals are made; it consists of cells

titanium (Ti, atomic no. 22) element, a light, strong metal; used in alloys for high-performance aircraft; titanium oxide (TiO_2) is made into white paint

titration finding the strength of a solution by reacting it with a solution of known strength

TNT trinitrotoluene ($CH_3C_6H_2(NO_2)_3$), an explosive

tomography method of X-raying a person where computers are used to build up a picture of cross section, like a slice through the body

torque two equal forces side by side in opposite directions, producing a twisting effect

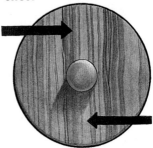

torsion strain produced by torque; how far something turns when it is twisted

total internal reflection reflection of light inside a piece of glass, etc., with no light escaping to the outside (for examples see critical angle, fibre optic)

toxic poisonous

trace element element of which a plant or animal needs a very small amount to stay healthy; for example people need a little iron in their food

trachea windpipe; tube through which an animal breathes

tracer (radioactive) small, harmless amount of radioactive element added to food or injected into the bloodstream, which can then be tracked from outside to see where the food or blood goes

trajectory path taken by a projectile

trans- in front of a word means 'through'

transducer device for converting a signal from one form to another, for example a microphone (sound into electricity) or a loudspeaker (electricity into sound)

transformer device for changing voltage of electricity

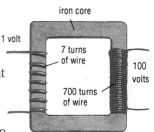

iron core
1 volt
7 turns of wire
700 turns of wire
100 volts

transistor semiconductor device used in electronic circuits; it allows a small current to control the flow of a large one

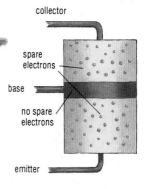

collector
spare electrons
base
no spare electrons
emitter

T

transition metals
large group of
elements, so called
because they make a
transition or bridge
between the two sides
of the periodic table

translucent letting
light through, but
not allowing a clear
image to be seen

transparent letting
light through and
allowing a clear
image to be seen

tri- in front of a word
means 'three'

triangulation
method of surveying
and mapmaking by
dividing land into
right-angled triangles

trigonometry
branch of mathematics
dealing with right-
angled triangles, used
in surveying; if you
know the length of
one side and the size
of one angle you can
work out the other
sides and angle by
using ratios known as

sine, cosine and
tangent, which are
listed in tables

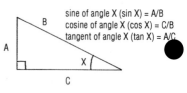

sine of angle X (sin X) = A/B
cosine of angle X (cos X) = C/B
tangent of angle X (tan X) = A/C

To find the height of the tree (A) :

Look up tan 30° - it is 0.57735
If A/C = 0.57735 and C is 100m,
then A = 57.735m

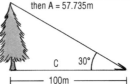

├── 100m ──┤

tritium isotope of
hydrogen with two
neutrons in the
nucleus as well as a
proton; used in fusion
reactions and also in
luminous paint,
because it glows

tropics two
lines around the
Earth 23 degrees
28 minutes north and
south of the equator,
the farthest north and
south where the Sun
can ever be directly
overhead (see axis)

tropism response of a plant to light or gravity, by growing towards or away from it

troposphere lowest layer of the atmosphere, up to about 15 km above the Earth; in this layer all the weather happens

tuber swelling on root of a plant in which it stores food for winter; for example a potato

tungsten (or wolfram, W, atomic no. 74) element, a metal with a very high melting point; used to make lightbulb filaments; tungsten carbide (WC) is very tough and used to make drills and grinding tools

tune to adjust to a certain frequency; for example tuning a radio receiver to the frequency of the radio waves broadcast by a particular station

turbine device in which a liquid or gas hits revolving blades and makes them turn

turbulence irregular, disorderly flow of a fluid (see laminar flow)

two-stroke engine engine in which the piston goes up and down once for every time the mixture explodes

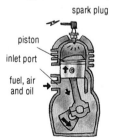

spark plug
piston
inlet port
fuel, air and oil

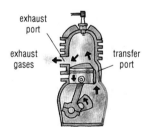

exhaust port
exhaust gases
transfer port

U

UHF ultra-high frequency, a radio waveband (see electromagnetic radiation)

UHT ultra-high temperature treatment to sterilize milk and cream; it is heated well above boiling point for a very short time

ultrasonic of sound: too high-pitched to hear (over 20,000Hz); ultrasonic waves can be used to 'see' inside the body, in much the same way as radar

ultra-violet radiation electromagnetic radiation with a wavelength slightly shorter than that of visible light (from about 10 nm to 500 nm); strong doses are harmful to living creatures

umbilical cord cord containing blood vessels by which the foetus of a mammal is fed by its mother; now also used to mean a cord used to supply electricity, a telephone link etc. to an astronaut on a space walk

umbra see penumbra

uncertainty principle problem in particle physics: you can measure either the position of a particle or its momentum, but not both

ungulate animal with hooves

uni- in front of a word means 'one'

unicellular having only one cell

unstable of an element: likely to decompose and therefore radioactive

uranium (U, atomic no. 92) element, a heavy radioactive metal; used as a fuel in atomic reactors and nuclear weapons; natural uranium is mostly the isotope uranium-238, but uranium-235 is needed for the fuel and has to be separated out

urine liquid in which waste products are sent out of the body

uterus hollow organ of female mammal in which young develop before birth

vaccine substance used to protect against disease: an injection of dead or weakened bacteria or viruses which make the body produce antibodies, so that when the real disease invades, it will be recognized and quickly attacked

vacuum empty space in fact there is no such thing; even in the space between the stars there is a little gas and dust

vacuum tube another name for a radio valve (in fact it contains gas at low pressure)

valency number of bonds an atom of a particular element can make (see bond), which depends on the number of electrons in its outer shell; some elements have more than one valency, which is written as a roman numeral: iron has a valency of 2 or 3, and oxygen has a valency of 2, so iron (II) oxide is FeO, iron (III) oxide is Fe_2O_3

valve anything that can be shut or opened to let something through; a radio valve is an old-fashioned device in which electricity flows in a controlled way through a gas, now mostly replaced by transistors

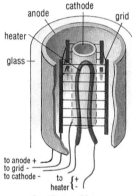

van de Graaff generator device for producing static electricity at a very high voltage

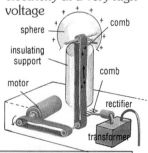

vanadium (V, atomic no. 23) element, a hard metal; used in steel to make a very tough alloy

vapour gas at a temperature low enough to allow it to be turned into a liquid without cooling it; there is water vapour in the air

variable quantity that changes in a mathematical calculation

variable geometry of an aircraft: having movable wings which can be swept back for high-speed flight and stretched out sideways for take-off and landing

vascular to do with tubes carrying fluid; an example of a vascular system is the veins and arteries of an animal

vector (biology) creature which carries the organism which causes a disease; mosquitoes are the vector of malaria because they carry the Plasmodium micro-organism which is the actual 'germ' of malaria

vector (physics) measurement for which you have to state the direction: speed is just speed, but velocity is speed in a certain direction, so velocity is a vector

vein blood vessel carrying blood back to the heart

velocity speed in a particular direction

venturi open-ended tube with narrow part in the middle, used to measure speed of flow of a fluid: the fluid speeds up as it goes through the narrow section, which makes its pressure fall; measuring the pressure tells you the speed

vernier device to make it easier to read a scale on a measuring instrument accurately

vertebra one of the bones in the backbone

vertebrate animal with backbone

vestigial existing as a small remainder or trace; you have a vestigial tail made of a few small bones at the base of your spine

VHF very high frequency, a radio waveband (see electromagnetic radiation)

video- in front of a word means 'seeing'

V

virus tiny object, not really a living thing, which causes disease by injecting DNA or RNA into a cell, which forces the cell to make new copies of the virus; a computer virus is a program which inserts information into other programs so that they make copies of the virus program, and may also annoy the user with silly messages or destroy parts of the computer's memory

viscosity friction inside a fluid, so that it does not flow easily; honey has a higher viscosity than water

vitamin substance of which you have to eat small amounts fairly often in order to stay healthy; the various vitamins (A, several B vitamins, C, D, E and K) are very different from each other, but all are needed to keep some process in the body going

viviparous giving birth to live young, rather than laying eggs

volatile of a liquid: easily turning to a vapour; volatile liquids often have a strong smell because of the vapour drifting around

volt (V) unit used to measure how much force an electric current has

voltage difference in electric charge between two points, so that if they are connected into a circuit a current will flow

voltmeter instrument used to measure voltage

volume amount of space something takes up

VTOL vertical take-off and landing

vulcanization hardening rubber and making it last longer by heating it with sulphur

waste products
unwanted products
of a process (for
example, digestion
or an industrial
process), which have
to be got rid of

**water of
crystallization** water
which forms part of
the structure of some
crystals, for example
washing soda
(sodium carbonate,
$Na_2CO_3.10H_2O$)

water table level
below which the
ground is saturated
with water; where the
water table is above
ground level there is
a pond or lake

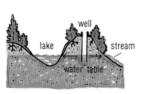

watt (W) unit of
electric power; found
by multiplying voltage
of a current by its
amperage

wattmeter
instrument for
measuring watts

wave any repeated
up-and-down, side-
to-side or to-and-fro
motion: light waves
are 'transverse' -
they vibrate at right
angles to the direction
they travel in but
sound waves are
'longitudinal' - air
molecules vibrate
to and fro along the
direction of travel

waveband range
of radio wavelengths;
for example, in
Britain the UHF
waveband is used for
television broadcasting
(see electromagnetic
radiation)

wavelength length
of a wave from
peak to peak (see
electromagnetic
radiation for examples)

wax beeswax and
vegetable waxes are
mixtures of esters;
paraffin wax is a
hydrocarbon

W

weight force with which the Earth (or wherever you are) attracts a certain mass (on the Moon you have the same mass but only weigh one sixth of your Earth weight)

on Earth   on the Moon

mass   weight   mass   weight

weightlessness state of an object when gravity is cancelled out by a force in the opposite direction; an astronaut in orbit is weightless because gravity is cancelled by centrifugal force

welding joining two pieces of metal by heating them so that they melt together; extra metal of the same kind may be added to strengthen the joint

white blood cell any of several kinds of cell in the blood (they are colourless, not really white) which protects you against disease

white light light of all colours mixed together

wind tunnel tunnel for aerodynamic testing of small models of aircraft, cars etc.; large fans blow air down it at high speed

wire recorder early form of tape recorder using steel wire instead of tape; very tough, and so still used for aircraft flight recorders which have to survive a crash

wolfram another name for tungsten

work movement caused by a force over a certain distance; measured in joules (1 joule is the work done by 1 newton over 1 metre)

wrought iron iron containing very little carbon; soft and easily magnetized

X axis on a graph, etc., direction from one side of the page to the other

X-rays electromagnetic radiation with wavelength between 0.01 nm and 10 nm; given off by radioactive elements, goes straight through light objects, so can be used to make photographs of inside of the body; large doses are harmful

xenon (Xe, atomic no. 54) element, a heavy inert gas; used in powerful fluorescent lamps, for example in cinema projectors

Xerox trade name of photocopier in which image is thrown on to a metal drum charged with electricity; bright parts of the image destroy the charge; black powder clings to the parts which are still charged; the powder is transferred to paper to make the print

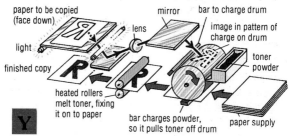

paper to be copied (face down)
mirror
bar to charge drum
image in pattern of charge on drum
lens
light
toner powder
finished copy
heated rollers melt toner, fixing it on to paper
bar charges powder, so it pulls toner off drum
paper supply

Y

Y axis on a graph, etc., direction from bottom of the page to top

yeast single-celled, fungus-like organism which eats sugar and gives off alcohol and carbon dioxide; used to produce alcoholic drinks and to make bread rise (because of the gas it makes)

Y

ytterbium (Yb, atomic no. 70) element, a metal

yttrium (Y, atomic no. 39) element, a metal

Z

Z axis on a graph, etc., drawn in 3D, direction that seems to be coming out of the page straight at you

zenith point in the sky directly over your head

zeolite mineral (natural or synthetic) with a spongy structure, very absorbent; used in many chemical processes including water softening

zinc (Zn, atomic no. 30) element, a metal; used as rustproof coating for steel, in batteries, and alloyed with copper to make brass

zirconium (Zr, atomic no. 40) element, a metal with a high melting point; used to make parts of jet engines and nuclear reactors

zoom lens complex camera lens whose focal length can be adjusted, so you can change the size of the picture

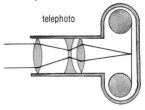

telephoto

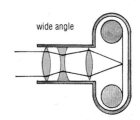

wide angle